Resting on His Promises

I am *Covered* from A to Z

LAURETHA WARD

Resting on His Promises: I Am Covered from A to Z
By: Lauretha Ward
Copyright © 2016, Lauretha Ward

ISBN-10: 1-939654-85-8
ISBN-13: 978-1-939654-85-4

All rights reserved solely by the author under international Copyright Law. Except where designated, the author certifies that all contents are original and do not infringe upon the legal rights of any other person or work. No part of this book may be reproduced in any form without the expressed written permission of the publisher. The views expressed in this book are not necessarily those of the publisher.

Unless otherwise noted, all Scripture quotations taken from the Amplified Bible. Copyright © 2015 by The Lockman Foundation. Used by permission. www.Lockman.org.

Scripture quotations marked NKJV are taken from the New King James Version®. Copyright © 1982 by Thomas Nelson. Used by permission. All rights reserved.

Cover design and interior layout by:
Jennifer LuVert,
Forerunners Ink, LLC

Printed in the United States

10 9 8 7 6 5 4 3 2 1

Published by:
Life To Legacy, LLC
P.O. Box 57
Blue Island, IL 60406
www.Life2Legacy.com
877-267-7477

Contents

4
Acknowledgments

5
Foreword

6
Introduction

9
You Are Approved and Valued

31
I Choose to Forgive

42
God Gives Me Strength for Every Storm

67
Willing to Confront and Conquer My Enemy

89
You are Chosen by His Design

126
Epilogue

129
About the Author

Acknowledgments

To my husband Gary, sons Aaron and Laurence, a special thank you for your loving-kindness, being such strong supporters, and much appreciated hugs through this endeavor. You all gave me the time and quietness to get this completed and encouraged me in the process. And I appreciate you Gary covering me in prayer from start to finish for every aspect of this book (and the prophetic word).

Corliss Brown, my Mom has given me bountiful pearls of wisdom, continual encouragement, and counsel through many life lessons and for that I'm forever thankful and very grateful.

To my siblings, Corlette and George Brown, I love you and thank God for your support, and believe God's promise for us as a family.

My special thanks to Bishop Don W. Shelby Jr, and First Lady Bonita A. Shelby, my spiritual parents for your continual prayer covering, teachings, encouragement, and support. You all have released many words since I've been connected in this ministry to motivate, empower, and inspire me to draw closer to God and move toward my purpose in this season of my life. You have been an integral part in my understanding the grace, love, and light of Jesus that I'm able to share with many in the body of Christ and to those who are lost.

I thank and appreciate all of my many spiritual mentors and ministry heroes whom I have gleaned from over the years: Rev. B.T. Hopkins, Pastor Willie E. Sheard, Pastor Willie J. Powell, Bill Hamon, Joyce Meyer, Cindy Trimm, Charles and Frances Hunter, Ruth Ward Heflin, Cindy Jacobs, James Goll, and John Eckhardt just to name a few.

To all of my friends; co-workers; and the saints of Burning Bush International Ministries I am eternally grateful for all of your well-wishes, love, encouragement, and prayers.

Foreword

My first experience with Lauretha's writings was her daily post on social media. It was then, that I recognized that she has a special gift. Her writings have inspired thousands on social media and I am confident that this book will encourage millions all over the world. *Resting on His Promises* is superbly written and it is a practical piece of literature that is full of insightful gems to encourage its readers to never lose hope!

Bishop Don W. Shelby, Jr.

Introduction

Resting on His Promises takes us each from a place of trying to help God do His part in our lives. He hasn't asked for nor does He need our help. You know how we can get in the mix and make matters worse when we so call try to help God out. We are only to be obedient to God's will and purpose for what He has called us to do but not at the expense of rushing His timing. Often, we are going to go through a process as we allow God to work some issues out of us and deposit some good things in us. Remember how Abraham at an old age was impotent yet was given the promise that he would be the father of many nations? He, of course, initially tried to quicken the process by rushing ahead of God's timing to birth an illegitimate son by his handmaiden. Yet that did not void the promise God had given Him. How many of you have a promise from God that you have held onto for many years concerning your health, finances, children, or marriage? Well, be encouraged because now is not the time to throw in the towel. You have got to put your confidence and trust in someone that is greater than what you are facing right at this moment. Just as Abraham did who by sight saw his body in a weakened dead state but,

In hope against hope Abraham believed that he would become a father of many nations, as he had been promised [by God]: "SO [numberless] SHALL YOUR DESCENDANTS BE." Without becoming weak in faith he considered his own body, now as good as dead [for producing children] since he was about a hundred years old, and [he considered] the deadness of Sarah's womb. But he did not doubt or waver in unbelief concerning the promise of God, but he grew strong and empowered by faith, giving glory to God, being fully convinced that God had the power to do what He had promised.

Romans 4:18-21

Looking at the circumstances, you may not be able to see your children saved, your body made whole, getting the promotion you desire, or your marriage being restored. But God has some choice promises that He is well able to produce in your life if you believe. For no matter how many promises God has made, they are "Yes" in Christ. And so through Him, the "Amen" is spoken by us to the glory of God (2 Corinthians 1:20). What I love about His promises is that there is no striving to obtain them. We do not have to beg for them or work for them.

For the promise that he would be the heir of the world was not to Abraham or to his seed through the law, but through the righteousness of faith. For if those who are of the law are heirs, faith is made void and the promise made of no effect, because the law brings about wrath; for where there is no law there is no transgression. Therefore it is of faith that it might be according to grace, so that the promise might be sure to all the seed, not only to those who are of the law, but also to those who are of the faith of Abraham, who is the father of us all (as it is written, "I have made you a father of many nations") in the presence of Him whom he believed—God, who gives life to the dead and calls those things which do not exist as though they did.
Romans 4:13-17, NKJV

If you are a believer in Christ, then every promise in the Bible from Genesis to Revelation is yours. God, our spiritual father, has even given a promise for every letter of the alphabet…yes, He has got you covered from A to Z, my brothers and sisters. As you begin to pour through the pages of this book, I encourage you to re-think and begin to declare aloud with confidence the promises that you know that you know are yours to stand on. Many times we have not simply because we have not asked. Let's start declaring, decreeing, and calling those things that be not as though they were and refuse to back down until the manifestation of what you are believing God for. I'm going to share with you how I came to rest on His promises for different areas of my life through personal experience using the following themes: You are Approved and Valued; I Choose to Forgive; God Gives Me Strength for Every Storm; Willing to Confront and Conquer My Enemy; and You are Chosen by His Design.

The promises are given to us by God's grace, and we need only have faith to believe and rest on His established word. If God has said it, then the word is settled and established forever.

Rest

Part 1

You Are Approved and Valued

I AM ACCEPTED IN THE BELOVED

*To the praise of the glory of his grace,
wherein he hath made us accepted in the beloved.*
Ephesians 1:6, KJV

When I think about the awesomeness of God, I am enthralled in wonderment and immediately reflect upon what Scriptures tell us about His total knowledge and understanding of His people. In the Psalm 139, David writes, "O LORD, thou hast searched me, and known me. Thou knowest my downsitting and mine uprising, thou understandest my thought afar off. Thou compassest my path and my lying down, and art acquainted with all my ways. For there is not a word in my tongue, but, lo, O LORD, thou knowest it altogether." Wow! Since it was God who formed us in our mothers' wombs, He knows every intimate detail about us. He knows all about our weaknesses and strengths, victories and defeats, triumphs and failures.

The Bible also declares that God is the author and the finisher of our faith. As the divine author, God plots our lives in masterful detail. He orders our steps, and in the annals of heaven, He meticulously records every detail of our lives. Each phase of our lives begins a new chapter in our life's story, from the beginning, to the middle, and ultimately the end. With the child of God, "all things work together for the good" and none of God's stories ends like a Greek tragedy. God has promised, "He who has begun a good work in you will complete it..." (Philippians 1:6). Understanding that God knows everything about us can be a little unsettling, because it means He sees our good, our bad, and our ugly—all of it. He knows our flesh is weak and that we are easily enticed by those besetting sins. Even when we want to do right, we quickly end up doing or saying the wrong thing. Yet, lovingly, He remains merciful and faithful, knowing exactly what we can and cannot bear. He is keenly aware of how relentless the enemy is in using shame, guilt, and condemnation to get us to throw in the towel. Despite our missteps and the devil's snares, God continuously gives us the faith, grace, and strength to run the race set before us. Through this, God's unconditional love for us is demonstrated. Since God is love, meaning that love is the necessary essence of His eternal being, He can only love us within the context of never-ending, undying love.

Though we speak of the awesomeness of God's love, it is actually beyond our comprehension. We can compare it to the relationship between a parent and child. As a child, when you messed up and had to humbly apologize to your parents, do you remember how they forgave you and gave you another chance? How much more will your heavenly Father, who is rich in mercy, forgive you? He will never give up on us despite our many downfalls and struggles. He is a compassionate, forgiving, and merciful God who will not toss us into a trash bin whenever we make a mistake.

On the other hand, it is the enemy of our souls, that wicked accuser, who wants to trip us up and see us condemned. I have a lot experience warring with the enemy. I know the devil's tactics from the many lies that he casts towards my mind. No, he doesn't play fair, but thank God we have the Helper, or the Holy Spirit, to lead and guide us into all truth. Certainly, the truth of His Word sets us free and causes us to triumph over the lies and schemes of the enemy.

When I look back over my life to when I was twelve years old, I remember attending a revival at my home church, Second Baptist. During the altar call, the revivalist gave the invitation to come to Christ. Suddenly, I felt a tugging at my heart to repent of my sins and accept Jesus into my heart as Lord and Savior. At the very second, I did so; I was accepted in the Beloved. I was saved. I became a member of the body of Christ. Through a divine operation of the Spirit, all of my sins—past, present, and future—had been nailed to the cross. These supernatural graces happened the minute I believed. Because I put my trust in Christ's finished work on Calvary's cross, I became a new creation in Christ Jesus: redeemed, sanctified, justified, and later to be glorified.

Did I understand fully what it meant to be saved at the time? No. And since all these spiritual realities took place, does it mean I have been faithful and committed since I asked the Lord to come into my heart? No. Have I been a perfect Christian since I confessed Christ? No, because I wavered in doubt, fear, and worry at times over circumstances in my life. Yes. Since I've been saved, I've messed up. I've been angry. I've not had the best attitude. I have not dotted every "i" nor crossed every "t" but in all of this I am not alone. The fact is, no Christian has been perfect. Christian maturity or sanctification is a lifelong process. All humans make mistakes.

Admittedly, I didn't always understand the truth about human weaknesses and frailties. It took years for me to finally come to grips with this fact. I was operating in a false identity belief system. I thought it was okay to be wired as independent and a perfectionist because I was following man-made standards. And I'll admit at times I've been stubborn and rebellious. I had to learn that my true identity is to be dependent on God, which is the only way to be a person of excellence. The "I gotta do it my way until I see it doesn't work" mindset has caused me a lot grief. Additionally, I know I cannot blame all my problems on the devil. I have learned to take responsibility for having gone left when God clearly told me to go right. I am, however, so extremely grateful that God is faithful and never wavers in His commitment to or love toward us.

Earlier I mentioned "the sins that so easily beset us." Therefore, we need to talk a little about sin. In the New Testament, the Greek word for "sin" is hamartia, which means "to miss the mark, to err, to fail of one's purpose." When you and I sin, we "miss the mark," or we fall short of God's standard. However, it's not only by sinning that we miss the mark. We fall short because since Adam's fall, we all have fallen natures; therefore, we fall short of God's holiness and righteousness no matter what we do. This is why even our self-righteousness doesn't count for anything. I praise God that though we are not perfect, we have a gracious Father who has made provisions for our sins and shortcomings through the shed blood of Jesus Christ.

God's love for us is so great that when Adam and Eve rebelled against Him in the Garden of Eden, He already had another plan in place. God expelled Adam and Eve from the Garden so they would no longer have access to the Tree of Life, which would have caused them to live forever in a sinful, unredeemable state. But the great act of grace is that humans can die, something angels and demons cannot do. However, when man sinned, God made a way of escape for him, and that was death. This set the stage for His only son "to die" for us to take away our sins at the predestined time. What a mighty God we serve! The devil thought he had us.

As the Scriptures declare, "He predestined and lovingly planned for us to be adopted to Himself as [His own] children through Jesus Christ, in accordance with the kind intention and good pleasure of His will—to the praise of His glorious grace and favor, which He so freely bestowed on us in the Beloved [His Son, Jesus Christ]" (Ephesians 1:5-6).

At one time or another, we have all looked for approval from others. Whether in academic achievement, athletic competition, or work performance, we all want to be approved and appreciated. Our need for acceptance and approval starts early in life, particularly during childhood. There is nothing more rewarding to a young child than hearing his father say, "Well done." Parents also love to see their children achieve. However, some parents fall into the trap of trying to live vicariously through their children. We have to leave room for our children to be themselves. Certainly, we all want our children to have a better life than we had and excel beyond what we were able to achieve. To ensure that, many parents will sacrifice by working overtime, taking on a second job, or maybe starting a part-time business just so their children can get a better start and go further in life than their parents.

This hustle-and-bustle world in which we live, is set up for us to receive recognition based on performance. But the concept of approval and recognition for performance sake often puts us in conflict with who we may actually be. At times, some of us have looked for validation from people before we come to understand what our purpose in life really is. Since people and the world around us so often change, we must find our approval and validation in the one constant that never changes—God. God so values us. We are so precious to Him that it doesn't matter what others say or think about you. So stop waiting to step out on what you are called to do because of others mere concept of what they think of you. And once you discover your purpose, do not let anyone limit or tell you what you cannot accomplish.

What matters most is that you are a person of extreme significance, approved of and valued by your heavenly Father. What God says about you is what matters the most. You are unique, beautiful, an extraordinary person valued and loved by God. This does not mean you will not have to work hard, increase knowledge, or continue to grow. You must continue to invest in improving yourself for the time you have in this life. It just means you don't need to live up to meeting others approval. You were predestined with the aim to please God and bring Him glory in the earth. Do not allow yourself to lose focus on that goal.

What about the shortcomings in our past? We must do what Paul says in Philippians, "Brothers and sisters, I do not consider that I have made it my own yet; but one thing I do: forgetting what lies behind and reaching forward to what lies ahead" (Philippians 3:13). Yes, we all have done things we are ashamed of, but as believers remember that our guilt, shame, and humiliation were nailed to the cross when we repented and asked for forgiveness. We leave the past in the past with no condemnation. What took place yesterday doesn't define our tomorrow! We must completely let it go and keep pressing into the call and purpose of our future. God is behind the scenes working together all things—including the bad—for your good. Therefore, press forward in the full assurance of His power and wisdom. Know that you can do all things through Christ who strengthens you. Keep moving forward and get it done! We have a great cloud of witnesses that are cheering us all in the game of life to cross the finish line.

Therefore, since we are surrounded by so great a cloud of witnesses [who by faith have testified to the truth of God's absolute faithfulness], stripping off every unnecessary weight and the sin which so easily and cleverly entangles us, let us run with endurance and active persistence the race that is set before us (Hebrews 12:1).

Prayer of Affirmation

I am a masterpiece handcrafted by God. I am created with purpose, and I am stepping out to do all that God has deposited in me. I am a person of extreme significance, approved of and valued greatly by my Father. I am loved unconditionally by God, and nothing in life or no one—no thing or no person—can ever separate me from His love. He loves me completely. I am the apple of His eye. I am accepted in the Beloved. (Ephesians 1:6, Deuteronomy 32:10, Romans 8:35-39)

I AM BLESSED AND HIGHLY FAVORED OF THE LORD

*And coming to her, the angel said,
"Greetings, favored one! The Lord is with you."
(Luke 1:28)*

Are you currently in a hard place? Hard places are those difficult times that stretch you to the hilt, where you are in over your head and your faith is tested to the uttermost. Hard places are circumstances like bankruptcy, foreclosure, eviction, terminal illness, unemployment, or underemployment, divorce, physical pain, a rebellious child, the ending of a relationship, and so on. You know that you are blessed (favored of God), but your current circumstances don't say or look like it. No matter what, you've got to hold on to your faith. Though it is easier said than done, hold on because the blessing is in the "going through." That's why we cannot base our current situation on what we see or feel. All of the distractions that come to take your eyes off the prize must be filtered out.

Yes, it can be disheartening trying to figure out how we are going to make it through another trial. In these situations we have to shift our focus and see the bigger picture through the grace and strength of Christ. Such was the case with Joseph. We see in Genesis 39, that Joseph (although a slave) was favored by his master because he recognized that the Lord was with Joseph. Doesn't that sound like a contradiction? How can a man be a slave and be favored by God at the same time? Here is what the Bible says, "The LORD was with Joseph, and he [even though a slave] became a successful and prosperous man; and he was in the house of his master, the Egyptian." (Genesis 39:2). The operative phrase here is, But the Lord was with Joseph. Even though Joseph was serving as a slave, the Lord was with him, and he was recognized as a prosperous and successful man.

Even when we are at our lowest point and trapped in a pit of despair, we can rest assured that the Lord is with us. God sees us from His perspective. God says, "Let the weak say, I am strong" (Joel 3:10). Let the poor say, "I am rich." Let the sick say, "I am healed." We must declare what the Word says about us: call it like you want to see it until you see it like you call it. God sees us as prosperous and successful from the time He fashioned us in our mother's womb.

Here is what God said to Abraham,

[A]s it is written [in Scripture], "I HAVE MADE YOU A FATHER OF MANY NATIONS") in the sight of Him in whom he believed, that is, God who gives life to the dead and calls into being that which does not exist.
Romans 4:17

None of us knows what goes on behind the scenes in our lives. Thank God, there are some people in our lives we can be transparent with, because they have been graced to deal with us. Not everyone can handle your humanness. For example, famous people are looked up to and even idolized, but trust me, they are just people; and if you get close enough to them, you'll find that out. Everyone has his or her shortcomings and weaknesses. Therefore, it is important to share your testimony about the weaknesses you have overcome, because you don't know who is struggling with the same thing from which you were delivered. In sharing your testimony, you also must use wisdom and discernment with what you say and how much you share because individuals are at different levels of maturity and may not be able to handle the real you.

Be wise. You cannot reveal all the nitty-gritty aspects of your struggles, even though you have been delivered for a long time. Since you cannot control how a person processes the information you download into his or her spirit, you must be prudent in what you disclose. You don't want to be become a stumbling block to someone else. Though you may go through hell and high water, be encouraged because what you are going through is not just for you. It is also for all of those you will help through your testimony. Therefore, you must endure hardness as a good soldier. Throwing in the towel and calling it quits is not an option.

There were times when situations arose where I wanted to say, "Really, this again? I thought I was over this situation. I thought I was finished with this struggle. Why do I have to go through this again?" It was tempting to just walk away from the things that were causing me pain. If I knew it was going to be like this, I could have gone another way, or I could have just stayed in bed that day, but now I have someone else to deal with. As the saying goes, "I can do bad all by myself!"

After rehearsing everything that was wrong and having a pity party, I would eventually get up out of my doldrums. It may have taken me a minute because sometimes I felt that I just needed to get everything out by rehearsing and venting to God how I felt I was being mistreated. However, each time I would read a passage of Scripture, hear a message at church, or rehearse a prophetic word from my journal that would encourage me to not quit. I have to remind myself not to grow weary for I shall see the benefit at the appointed time.

One good thing about trouble is that it does not last. Though affliction is painful, it is working something in me and out of me that can bring glory to God. We are coming out better than we were before we went in because God gives us the strength to endure. Just like Joseph, we must know that all that we go through leads us to that defining moment when we walk out of our prison to the palace—destiny fulfilled.

FAVOR IS CONNECTED TO YOUR PURPOSE

Are you in a pit right now? Do not despair. That pit could actually be divinely connected to your purpose. When you have favor on your life, certainly you are going to face many pitfalls orchestrated by God that will eventually be stepping-stones out of that ugly pit. Here is what the Scriptures say:

Now his master saw that the LORD was with him and that the LORD caused all that he did to prosper (succeed) in his hand. So Joseph pleased Potiphar and found favor in his sight and he served him as his personal servant. He made Joseph overseer over his house, and he put all that he owned in Joseph's charge. It happened that from the time that he made Joseph overseer in his house and [put him in charge] over all that he owned, that the LORD blessed the Egyptian's house because of Joseph; so the LORD'S blessing was on everything that Potiphar owned, in the house and in the field.

Genesis 39:3-5

Joseph, who was hated by his brothers, was thrown into a pit to perish. But instead of letting him perish he was sold to a company of Ishmaelites who took him to Egypt where Pharaoh's captain of the guard, named Potiphar, purchased him as a slave. Potiphar was so pleased with Joseph that he elevated him to the position of overseer. The Lord blessed Potiphar's house because of Joseph's favor with God. Prosperity extended to all that Potiphar had in the house and in the field. God's favor on Joseph's life caused everything that he touched to prosper. Then one day Joseph was falsely accused of raping Potiphar's wife, after she tried to seduce him. Now Joseph goes from Potiphar's house to prison. Yet, God's favor remained on his life. Here is what the Scriptures say:

But the LORD was with Joseph and extended lovingkindness to him, and gave him favor in the sight of the warden. The warden committed to Joseph's care (management) all the prisoners who were in the prison; so that whatever was done there, he was in charge of it. The warden paid no attention to anything that was in Joseph's care because the LORD was with him; whatever Joseph did, the LORD made to prosper.
Genesis 39:21-23

This passage gives us hope. Environment and circumstances cannot hinder God's favor. Even in the midst of having haters, being wrongfully accused, and being forgotten or not appreciated, you are okay. You are divinely positioned to be where you are on purpose and for purpose. God sees it all, so never forget that what you are going through is a part of His plan for your life. Remember, the steps of a good man or woman are ordered by the Lord.

DON'T STOP SERVING WHILE IN YOUR PIT

Due to God's favor, Joseph was placed in authority over the other prisoners. However, Joseph had the gift of prophetic dreams, along with the ability to interpret dreams. It was this gift that brought him face-to-face with his destiny. Two years after interpreting a couple of dreams concerning two of his fellow inmates, Joseph was called upon to interpret a dream that troubled the Pharaoh. Then Pharaoh said to Joseph,

"Since [your] God has shown you all this, there is no one as discerning and clear-headed and wise as you are. You shall have charge over my house, and all my people shall [a]be governed according to your word and pay respect [to you with reverence, submission, and obedience]; only in [matters of] the throne will I be greater than you [in Egypt]." Then Pharaoh said to Joseph, "See, I have set you [in charge] over all the land of Egypt." Then Pharaoh took off his signet ring from his hand and put it on Joseph's hand, and dressed him in [official] vestments of fine linen and put a gold chain around his neck. He had him ride in his second chariot; and runners proclaimed before him, "[Attention,] bow the knee!" And he set him over all

the land of Egypt. Moreover, Pharaoh said to Joseph, "Though I am Pharaoh, yet without your permission shall no man raise his hand [to do anything] or set his foot [to go anywhere] in all the land of Egypt [all classes of people shall submit to your authority]."

Genesis 41:39-44

Joseph brought restoration to all of Egypt through divine wisdom and leadership that God taught him while going through his trials. After his elevation to second in command of Egypt, Joseph found himself over Potiphar, the man whom he served. His favor and his trials (betrayal, slavery, and imprisonment) were connected to his great purpose.

In another example, God's Son had favor that was connected to His purpose to be the Savior of the world. The Scriptures declare, "And Jesus kept increasing in wisdom and in stature, and in favor with God and men" (Luke 2:52). The Son of God had favor on His life. Yet He also endured suffering, rejection, pain, and even death.

[S]aying, "The Son of Man must suffer many things and be rejected [as the Messiah] by the elders and chief priests and scribes (Sanhedrin, Jewish High Court), and be put to death, and on the third day be raised up [from death to life]."

Luke 9:22

It really puts things in perspective to see that our Elder Brother was favored by God and man and yet suffered many things including betrayal, persecution, rejection, ridicule, pain, and death by crucifixion. And He, being our example, gives us a pattern of how to endure the vicissitudes of life, yet he did so without sin and was highly favored by the Father. This brings us to a point that cannot be over emphasized: just because we are blessed and highly favored of the Lord doesn't mean we get a pass on suffering. The Bible clearly teaches, "But may the God of all grace, who called us to His eternal glory by Christ Jesus, after you have suffered a while, perfect, establish, strengthen, and settle you" (1 Peter 5:10, NKJV).

As we go through our trials, some of us talk it out, shout it out, pray it out, fast it out, praise it out, or cry it out. The choice is up to us as to how we go through our trouble. No matter which course of action you take, one thing is certain: God is only moved by faith. When we are going through, we must learn to stand on His promises and practice speaking what God says in His Word. Just as David did, encourage yourself in the Lord with these scriptural affirmations:

> "The joy of the Lord is my strength."
> "I am blessed and highly favored of the Lord."
> "All things are working together for my good."

There is purpose in the pain and power in His plan. God is very intentional. Everything He does and allows is on purpose. He knows (even when we don't) exactly how much we can bear, He will not allow the enemy to tempt us beyond our capability, and finally, He will provide a way of escape.

I am not perfect. I have flaws, make mistakes, and have fallen into some miry pits of my own creation. However, I continue to walk by faith until I see the manifestation of what God has promised me. That's the word, and I am prophesying and sticking to it. Even when I have bouts of fear and doubt, I hold fast to what God's Word promises. How do we get out of the pits of despair we have created? Certainly, it is not by doing things our way. However, through the purity of heart we follow the path of God's Word, which will guide us in the right direction.

The steps of a [good and righteous] man are directed and established by the LORD, And He delights in his way [and blesses his path]. Establish my footsteps in [the way of] Your word; Do not let any human weakness have power over me [causing me to be separated from You].

Psalm 37:23; 119:133

In June 1998, I attended one of the most powerful women's retreats I have ever experienced. While there, a woman named Lydia Clarke gave me a prophetic word. Here is what she prophesied: "You will war—your weapon is your pen—demons will tremble when you pick up a pen. You tear down kingdoms. Your writings will be in other countries. As you go through adversities write. Pick up your pen. People will be delivered through your writings." Shortly after that, I published two books; but I put down my pen and didn't move forward to write and release the other books. Then the prophetic word resurged in my spirit, and I began reworking the manuscript I started in 2012. Oddly, things kept being stalled behind the scenes with the publishing company—or so I thought. These obstacles I was encountering were all part of God's plan because the Lord wanted me to release a new book through a different company. It came with a prophetic word released by my pastor, Don W. Shelby, Jr., in January 2014. He prophesied, "Memoirs, memoirs, memoirs. I have placed a book inside of you and it will be released in paperback to the nations." Following the unction for me to attend a service that Pastor Shelby was speaking at in Flint, Michigan, I asked God specifically to give me a word regarding my book. The confirmation came during the summer of 2015. At the end of his message, Pastor Shelby prophesied to me, saying, "God has given you the green light to go write your book." And just as 2 Chronicles 20:20b says, "Believe and trust in the LORD your God and you will be established (secure). Believe and trust in His prophets and succeed," I believed the word the Lord had spoken through His prophet.

This time something sparked within that with God helping me, I was going to complete the book. However, it would be necessary to yield to God moving on me to write. I had to let go and let God lead me. It was time to stop over thinking how I was going to get it done. I simply had to do it. Even though I'm wired to want to know all of the details upfront before I make a move, I eventually realized that that's not faith, and without faith it is impossible to please God (Hebrews 11:6). I finally came to grips with the fact that I'm not alone; I also realize this is a faith walk, and that God was repositioning me for a new assignment. As I began to take the initial steps to write, I rested in God knowing that He would order all of my steps.

I've noticed that there is a flow and an ease now that I have realigned myself with God's will and purpose for my life. At this point, let me ask you some key questions. Are you struggling with getting out of the pit to realign yourself with God's purpose? Are you afraid of the unknown? Would you have to step outside of your comfort zone? If you answered "yes" to any of these questions, welcome to the faith zone! Yep! It's outside of your comfort zone where you are going to find success. Take a risk! Be encouraged knowing that the favor and blessing of God for your life are connected to His designed purpose. He will be right there with you to guide you every step of the way. I'm not suggesting that it is going to be easy, but it will be worth it. The bottom line is, it's a matter of trusting that He knows what is best for us.

FAVOR IS CONNECTED TO YOUR PROMISE

It doesn't matter if you are in the back of the line; your current position in life does not dictate or negate your promise or purpose. Remember Joseph's story? In Genesis 39 he was a slave who had been betrayed and lied upon. However, two chapters later, Joseph had been promoted to the front of the line. He was taking orders from Potiphar in Genesis 39, and was giving orders to Potiphar in Genesis 41. How did it happen? God's Favor! You may be in the back of the line, taken for granted, marginalized, and overlooked today, but continue to serve and be faithful. You will not remain in the back of the line for ever. Though it may tarry, hold on, your break through is coming. God will cause you to move up in positions even though you may not have the education, years of experience, or status in the eyes of people. One thing to remember, favor is not fair. By definition, fair means that everyone is to be treated the same. That's why I don't want God's fairness; I want His favor. Favor looks beyond my faults and frailties and propels me ahead of others all because God has placed His favor upon me.

Here is some wisdom: recognize that the greater the opposition you face in your life the likelihood that it is working in your favor to bring forth a greater level of glory. People who don't like you don't even have a clue that they are really blessing you. Let them talk because they will actually be unknowingly prophesying your future declaring who they think you are by what they perceive about you. God is using your trials to work out for your good. Knowing this will help you develop a foundation for remaining cool, calm, and collected in the face of those who come against you or despitefully use you. Joseph did not go after his brothers for how they mistreated him because he knew that what they meant for evil God meant for good.

Prayer of Affirmation
What the enemy has meant for my bad God is turning around for my good. All things are working together and are fitting into a plan for good to me and for me because I love God and I am called according to His design and purpose. When trouble arises,

I can go through it with the joy of the Lord as my strength. I will come out of the pitfalls that will lead to my stepping-stones. I am increased in wisdom, in stature and years, and in favor with God and man. I am blessed and highly favored of the Lord. (Genesis 50:20, Romans 8:28, Nehemiah 8:10, Luke 2:52, Luke 1:28)

I AM COMPLETE IN HIM

And in Him you have been made complete [achieving spiritual stature through Christ], and He is the head over all rule and authority [of every angelic and earthly power].
Colossians 2:10

Do you sometimes struggle with feeling less-than, as if you don't count or matter? Have you ever felt that you don't measure up or fit in with a particular group? Do you think in some way you are missing something in your capabilities or you are tormented by some personality trait that causes you to be self-conscious and overcritical of yourself? Do you say things like:

I'm too light. I'm too dark. I'm too skinny. I'm too fat. I'm too short. I'm too tall. I'm not smart enough. I'm stupid. I'll never get married because nobody wants me. I have too many freckles—or whatever. The question is, Why are you criticizing yourself? What's wrong is not you. Besides, whose standards are you to measure up to anyway? Who says you are to look or be a certain way? Oftentimes, we compare ourselves to what we see on television or in magazines, not to mention what's out there in social media and Hollywood. In trying to keep up with societal trends, we make adjustments to keep up with someone else's image. Doing this causes so much anxiety because when we try to adapt to someone else, we lose our true identity.

That is not by God's design. We are easily frustrated with trying to look like, act like, and do like somebody else, which in most cases is a false image anyway. Trying to keep up with being someone you are not causes you to have low self-esteem and will leave you broke or broken, fearful, frustrated, empty, and exhausted. How can we be who God has created us to be attempting to follow the dictates of other people's lives? Instead of finding liberation, we would only end up in bondage because we cannot experience true freedom in trying to be someone else. We would only lose our identity, uniqueness, and authenticity.

ADJUST YOUR MIND'S LENS

During my teen years, I struggled with being short. The fact that I was 5'2" and the shortest among my peers led to my having low self-esteem. I so badly wanted to be taller. To compensate for being vertically challenged, I would always look for shoes with heels two inches or more to add to my height. Though no one has ever told me that I am too short, back in the fifth grade my best friend nicknamed me "Wee." She was not ridiculing or belittling me, but she didn't realize her pet name for me played into my insecurity about my height. "I'm too short" is what I constantly told myself. It's not what people say to us that is most damaging, but it's what we tell ourselves that makes all the difference in the world. If we could control the messaging of the inner voice, we can change the perception of ourselves. To be truly free on the outside, we must be liberated on the inside in order to live our best life now. We were created as an original; therefore, we must silence the voice of self-conscious criticisms that wage war in our minds. Yes, there is a war going on in the battlefield of the mind.

The part of the body the enemy wants more than anything else is between your two ears. By default, we yield our minds to him when we choose to focus on the wrong things. The only way to change our perspective is by adjusting our mind's lens. Too much focus can be spent on magnifying our inadequacies. God made us unique and beautiful just as we are. Therefore, we need to shift our focus and start repeating to ourselves the good things God has declared about us. Our creator doesn't make any mistakes. We should never feel as though we are "less than" in any area of our lives. Apart from Him, we gain the wrong perspective and consequently see ourselves as not measuring up. This is how we fall short of attaining all that He has purposed for our lives.

There have been times when I have been hesitant to step out on faith when asked to do something. My thought process would be *"There are others who can do that better than me."* Insecurity would also have me questioning myself. *"What if I make a mistake?" "What if I'm a big failure?"* I often started a ping-pong match with my thoughts going back and forth about how I didn't measure up. That was my internal processes, but how do others think? Another person's views may fluctuate too, based on the emotional, spiritual, and physical conditions they are experiencing at the time. If we are not careful, our desire to please others will diminish our desire to please God. Such was the case when several years ago I was asked to speak for a women's program. I didn't even want to consider doing it because I was afraid with having to get up in front of all those people in the church. The next thought was What will I say? Initially, my response to the invitation was no. However, I could not shake it. I remember waking up one morning with a stiff neck. I can recall hearing in my spirit that I was being stiff-necked and rebellious. I was praying early that morning and I repented. I said to the Lord, "I can't do this on my own, and if Holy Spirit will be right there with me to give me what to say, then I will speak for the women's program." Immediately after that, the pain in my neck was gone. I reasoned with myself that it was no different from teaching a class of thirty students. It was just a bigger audience. My fear-induced doubt was replaced with faith-induced confidence, godly confidence. I felt a peace and assurance that Holy Spirit would guide me and tell me what to say.

At times, we need to reposition the lens, shifting it off what we cannot do and focusing on the fact that we can do all things through Christ who strengthens us. In Him we move, live, and have our being. We can do more than we know with His help as we call on Him and trust Him to do greater works in us and through us. We can't allow external circumstances, our past, or people to contradict our internal belief system. God didn't create you to be like anyone else in the world. You are a unique, handcrafted design of your Creator. As stated in Genesis, "So God created man in His own image, in the image and likeness of God He created him; male and female He created them" (Genesis 1:27). This means that His DNA is inside of you. You have a deposit of greatness, power, strength, wisdom, loving-kindness, and goodness within you. Therefore, you are fully equipped and qualified to do whatever He calls you to do. As His beloved children, we have to allow His Word to renew our minds so we can hear what "thus saith the Lord" concerning our true identity and purpose.

We are not lacking broken misfits to God. According to His word, we are complete, which means we have all the necessary parts and are whole to be and do what He has purposed for our lives. The Bible says: "And in Him you have been made complete [achieving spiritual stature through Christ], and He is the head over all rule and authority [of every angelic and earthly power]" (Colossians 2:10).

Prayer of Affirmation

I am who God says I am. I can do all things through Christ who gives me strength. I am beautiful. I will praise You, for I am fearfully and wonderfully made. I have been chosen for greatness. I carry God's DNA of greatness, power, strength, loving-

kindness, and goodness inside of me. I am a unique, bold, and brave individual. I am fully equipped to carry out my God-given assignment with a spirit of wisdom and excellence. And the Spirit of the LORD rests upon me—the spirit of wisdom and understanding, the spirit of counsel and might, the spirit of knowledge and of the fear of the LORD. I am whole and complete in Him. (Philippians 4:13, Psalm 139:14, Isaiah 11:2)

D

I AM DEFENSIVELY CLAD WITH THE ARMOR OF GOD

Therefore, put on the complete armor of God, so that you will be able to [successfully] resist and stand your ground in the evil day [of danger], and having done everything [that the crisis demands], to stand firm [in your place, fully prepared, immovable, victorious].
Ephesians 6:13

At one time or another, we are all faced with a crisis, challenge, and hardship. Maybe the challenge is an ultimatum you received in a relationship. Or maybe abrupt changes at work have occurred, and now you are confronted with being relocated or downsized out of a job. Maybe you have received some unexpected bad news concerning yours or a loved one's health that shakes you to the core. Whatever the circumstances, we all experience our share of problems, challenges, and upsets. Initially, we may experience a range of feelings and ride the roller coaster of emotions, up and down with fear, frustration, and anger. But no matter what, we know that we can't wallow in self-pity or throw in the towel because it won't do us or those around us any good.

MIRACLE IN THE MAKING

On March 16, 2001, I was handed a letter that stated,

```
It has come to our attention that your certificate of
clinical competency has expired as of 12/31/00. This
certification is required to maintain your employment.
Please be advised that a copy of current certification
must be presented to your current supervisor and/or
manager by 3/31/01. If compliance with this request
cannot be met within the time frame, our facility
will have no choice but to suspend your employment
until current documentation is presented, based on
Policy #518.
```

After the supervisor left the room, I went through a range of emotions while reading the letter. I made the foolish mistake of not being recertified prior to it expiring. But as I was getting ready to call the ASHA (American Speech-Hearing Association) to make a payment for the license I heard in my spirit No weapon formed against you shall prosper. I called ASHA and made a payment by phone and was informed that the card would arrive in the mail in 3-4 weeks. That would put me past the deadline of when they wanted me to have the actual documentation. I asked God for a miracle because I needed the card to arrive before March 31. The Lord gave me another Scripture of comfort, "Do not be afraid! Take your stand [be firm and confident and undismayed] and see the salvation of the LORD which He will accomplish for you today; for those Egyptians whom you have seen today, you will never see again. The LORD will fight for you while you [only need to] keep silent and remain calm" (Exodus 14:13-14). I held on to that Scripture, so confident the Lord was coming through for me that I boasted about what He was going to do with my Sunday school class. On March 18, I told them I was expecting a miracle and would receive my card before March 31. Now of course there was a spiritual battle going on within me, but I refused to give in. Every day I would get out of my car to go into the building reciting the Word the Lord had given me, "No weapon formed against me shall prosper. I have no fear. I am confident that I will see the salvation of the Lord. I will receive my card in the mail before March 31. The Lord will fight for me and I shall hold my peace and remain at rest." I continued to do that throughout the day, and it kept me settled and reassured so that I could get through my workday peacefully.

As the time drew closer to the deadline, on March 27 my supervisor asked me for the card because I was going to be out of town and wasn't going to return until the beginning of April. I told her I didn't have it yet and would let her know on Wednesday before I left to go on vacation. When I hung up the phone after talking with her, I immediately said, "Lord, I am standing on your word. No weapon formed against me shall prosper. I have no fear. There is a ram in the bush, and the card is on the way before the thirty-first."

My supervisor called me back five minutes later to say she had called ASHA and was informed that my membership was paid through December 2001. Therefore, I could come into work Monday and bring a copy whenever the card came. That was fine, but I was still waiting for my card to show up before March 31 because that was what I had asked of God. I arrived back in town Sunday, April 1 at 3:00 a.m. and picked up my mail. Before I went through the stack, I said, "Thank you for the card." Going through the envelopes, I began to smile as I saw it had arrived at my home on March 29. God did it! I was able to return to work with a copy in my hand to give my supervisor that Monday. I couldn't stop smiling, as she was shocked that I had received it so soon. It was a wonderful feeling; words cannot adequately express what this miracle meant to me. Have you ever had one of those moments when all you could say to the enemy, "Thought he had me ... but God"?

Prayer of Affirmation
I expect a miracle today. I put on the whole armor of God so I can resist the enemy and stand firm on Your word. No weapon formed against me shall prosper in my life. I have no fear. I shall stand on your word. I am confident that I will see the salvation of the Lord. The Lord will fight for me and I shall hold my peace and remain at rest.
(Ephesians 6:13, Isaiah 54:17, Exodus 14:13-14)

Rest

Part 2

I CHOOSE TO FORGIVE

I AM THE ELECT OF GOD

So, as God's own chosen people, who are holy [set apart, sanctified for His purpose] and well-beloved [by God Himself], put on a heart of compassion, kindness, humility, gentleness, and patience [which has the power to endure whatever injustice or unpleasantness comes, with good temper].
Colossians 3:12

Have you ever gotten tired of waiting on something to come through for you such as a promotion on your job? Are you trying to fix something in your relationship, but instead of it getting better it seems to be getting worse? Has someone ever pushed your button that you began to wonder how are you going to maintain your temper let alone your choice of words? Let's pause right here on that last question. According to Proverbs 18:21, "death and life are in the power of the tongue." The tongue is powerful because it can speak blessings or curses, life or death. If it were possible to replay some of the harsh things we have said to others, we may find that we have set death or curses in motion on our family, friends, and even ourselves. This occurs because we readily speak negativity to situations we are going through at the time.

In the heat of the moment, we can be abrasive and condescending toward others, setting the spiritual principles of the spoken word into action. The verbal seeds we sow into the atmosphere we definitely began to reap those things in our lives. Imagine a person whenever they see a particular individual saying under their breathe "ooh you make me sick to my stomach." Do you wonder why that person has a digestive disorder? The man that constantly says "my boss is a pain in my neck" and doesn't understand why he now has been struggling with being unable to turn his head due to neck pain. What about the woman who complains about her ex-husband "is a pain in the butt" and she is battling hemorrhoids. You have a girlfriend with twin toddlers who repeatedly states, "These kids are driving me up a wall and keep getting on my last nerves," now she finds herself being confused, forgetful, and misplacing items. Lastly, the single mom who is struggling with raising her teenage son says, "Boy you're never going to amount to anything; you'll end up being just like your no-good daddy." Lo and behold, by the time Johnny turns 18, he ends up in jail just like his father.

These are the negative effects of letting our emotions get the best of us without taking heed to God's Word, which says:

Understand this, my beloved brothers and sisters. Let everyone be quick to hear [be a careful, thoughtful listener], slow to speak [a speaker of carefully chosen words and], slow to anger [patient, reflective, forgiving].

James 1:19

HEALTHY WORDS BRING VICTORY

Healthy words are powerful because they act as change agents. An example of healthy words are confessing your faults and praying for one another. That's when healing can occur. Someone coined the phrase "Expose the devil and he'll go, but if you hide him, he'll grow." I like to say, "Keep it real and be healed." Now I have been guilty just as anyone else has of murmuring and complaining. As a result, I ended up in the midst of a test of my own.

Many years ago, I received a low rating on my performance appraisal from my manager due to there being a 23-point drop from the previous year. I explained to my manager that I was not in agreement with the rating and she stated, "Well it's average; you got a standard rating." Though I really didn't agree with her explanation, I decided to sign off on the report anyway. However, I couldn't let it go so I went over her head to Human Resources. They in turn had her to re-do it with me giving validation as to why the numbers should be increased. Even with some of the points being increased, I still was not satisfied with the overall rating. So I decided to take matters into my own hand. I made an appointment to talk to her manager who is the head of administration. I figured that I would definitely have the last say and that she would be reprimanded.

THE BATTLE IS THE LORD'S

It is interesting how worked up over this situation I had become. What was really happening is that the enemy was waging a spiritual attack against me that I was trying to fight in the flesh. I gave the enemy an opening in my defenses because my feelings were hurt and I was offended. Scripture is clear in such incidents. The Bible says:

For our struggle is not against flesh and blood [contending only with physical opponents], but against the rulers, against the powers, against the world forces of this [present] darkness, against the spiritual forces of wickedness in the heavenly (supernatural) places.

Ephesians 6:12

I was armed and ready to go into the administrator's office with my report, but before I did that I prayed on the day of the scheduled appointment. Unfortunately, my last resort should have been my first resort. I should have started warfare prayer when the manager initially handed me the performance appraisal, but instead I chose to put the spotlight on her flaws without owning up to my part in this whole situation. However, doing it on my own made my flesh feel good and fed into my pride, even though God wanted to work out His plan in my life. After coming to my senses, I prayed and asked God what I should do. The Lord spoke to my heart and said, "Do not repay evil for evil, overcome evil with good. Show her acts of kindness. Send flowers and cards for encouragement. Vengeance is mine, and I will repay."

I couldn't believe it that after everything I rehearsed in my mind and written down on paper to tell the manager, I'm to give her flowers? Can that be real? I was not thrilled with what I was told to do but I decided to be obedient. I made the choice to humbly submit to the Father with a repentant heart and did not give into Satan's attempts to control my mind to vindicate myself. Therefore, it says, "God is opposed to the proud and haughty, but [continually] gives [the gift of] grace to the humble [who turn away from self-righteousness]" (James 4:6b).

I went to my two co-workers and asked for their forgiveness for venting to them about the situation, and I purchased a bouquet of flowers and gave them to the manager. For the next eight months, until I went on maternity leave, I slipped a card with words of encouragement under her door. I did so with no expectation as she never thanked me for any of the cards. I also prayed for her daily and the Lord gave me a poem regarding the situation—instead of payback, pray back. In this test, my weapons of warfare were not carnal, but they are mighty through God to the pulling down of strongholds. I found myself over time no longer harboring bitterness, unforgiveness, or a negative attitude about the situation.

Many people commented on the fact that manager seemed to have had nine lives because there were others who sought retribution for how she treated them as well. However, because I was in relationship with God, I was held to a higher standard. When my co-workers wanted to talk negative about her, my response was "God bless her." Immediately, that would shut down any further backbiting. I had resolved in my heart that I was going to allow God to have full control in the situation. God allowed me to understand this important principle, that people who are hurting inside, tend to hurt other people. Knowing this gave me the insight to show compassion for her and put God's love in action.

Our failure to forgive creates a root of bitterness in our hearts that spreads like cancer. Bitterness kills your blessings, hinders your prayers, and blocks God from forgiving you. Unforgiveness is one of Satan's most potent weapons that he uses against believers. In 2 Corinthians 2:10-11, the Bible admonishes us to forgive: "If you forgive anyone anything, I too forgive [that one]; and what I have forgiven, if I have forgiven anything, has been for your sake in the presence of [and with the approval of] Christ, to keep Satan from taking advantage of us; for we are not ignorant of his schemes."

Unforgiveness will block God's love from entering our hearts. Our hearts began to become callous, bound by hurt and bruised emotions. Jesus came to free us from captivity by dying on the cross because of God's love for us. He came to heal and bind up the wounds from negative hurtful words that have pierced our hearts. And He wants us to forgive those who have hurt us knowingly and unknowingly. It is imperative that we be fully liberated and not allow any lurking bitterness to remain in our hearts. Only then can we be free to love as He loves.

If you try to think back on all that you have been forgiven for by our loving Savior, you couldn't do it because it is too numerous to recall. We have sinned so many times out of anger, pain, misunderstanding, fear, and trying to protect ourselves. Daily we miss the mark and thank God that He doesn't just kick us to the curb. The same holds true for those who have hurt us. They sinned out of hurt, pain, and ignorance. They have no idea of how greatly you would be impacted by the cruelty of their words or actions toward you. It takes them seeing from a different vantage point. Only then can we understand that we need to forgive others just as God has forgiven us. He is a God of mercy, forgiveness, compassion, and grace. Likewise, we should demonstrate Christ-like mercy to those who have offended us in order to grow in grace.

I went on maternity leave, and two weeks before I returned to work, I was informed that my manager was no longer there. She had been removed by administration and escorted off of the premises. What I didn't know is that behind the scenes my manager was being watched by administration and a case had been built against her starting around the time of my performance appraisal. God knew and was faithful to His word. In James, the Bible teaches, "So then, my beloved brethren, let every man be swift to hear, slow to speak, slow to wrath; for the wrath of man does not produce the righteousness of God" (James 1:19-20). It wasn't enough for me to know in my heart what the Lord was going to do but I also consistently spoke the Word regarding the situation.

When I returned to work, my new manager was someone I had worked closely with as a therapist prior to her promotion. She said, "I trust you to give an accurate assessment of your job performance." She was in agreement with my appraisal, and I received a decent pay increase. What a powerful lesson and test to learn patience, kindness, and forgiveness, and that when I hold my peace I can be at peace. As His chosen ones, He gives us the ability and strength to endure even when it appears we are wrongly suffering. Besides, God has his hosts of angels fighting on our behalf in the spiritual realm. We have already won the battle; we just must get the instructions for what our part is to be. The LORD says this to you: "Be not afraid or dismayed at this great multitude, for the battle is not yours, but God's" (2 Chronicles 20:15). Through that I learned a lesson: I had the power to choose therefore, I chose to forgive.

Prayer of Affirmation

Father, forgive me for times when I become hurt and frustrated and try to take matters into my own hands by blaming others. Help me to examine my heart and see where I am wrong. Open my eyes to see beyond my hurt. I make the choice to forgive. Thank You for giving me the strength and peace to forgive. Give me wisdom and direction as to what I must do. Help me to wait on your guidance and follow the details of the instruction with an obedient heart. Thank You for guiding me continually in the situation, even if it doesn't make sense in the natural. Thank You for peace that will keep guard over my heart, for it determines the course of my life. I have no fear of man or my enemies for the battle is not mine, but yours, Father. In Jesus' name, amen. (James 1:5, Isaiah 58:11, Proverbs 4:23, 2 Chronicles 20:15)

I AM FORGIVEN BECAUSE OF THE FINISHED WORK ON THE CROSS

When you were dead in your sins and in the uncircumcision of your flesh (worldliness, manner of life), God made you alive together with Christ, having [freely] forgiven us all our sins, having canceled out the certificate of debt consisting of legal demands [which were in force] against us and which were hostile to us. And this certificate He has set aside and completely removed by nailing it to the cross.
Colossians 2:13-14

Do you ever find yourself stumbling over the same things day after day, and year after year that you thought you would have been rid of by now? Why can't I get rid of the habit of lying? Why can't I stop being angry when he or she comes around? Why can't I just push back from overeating? Yes, I struggled with certain issues for years that would have me feeling guilty because I was bound by being a perfectionist. Trying to cross all of the t's and dot all of my i's thinking if I could do the right thing it would earn me brownie points with God. I would beat myself up when I didn't do or say the right thing. But the truth is you or I could never do anything through our own efforts to make ourselves righteous. The righteousness that counts is imputed (or put on our account) by God. Our best efforts to achieve righteousness are as filthy rags (Isaiah 64:6).

Just imagine Old Testament days when the people of God tried to follow the Law. The Law represented the old covenant agreement, and it was impossible for people to be holy and righteous. The purpose of the Law was to expose their sin. However, Jesus came and established a new order called grace. And it was at the cross of Calvary, where the sins of the whole world were transferred to Jesus, the Lamb of God, our sin offering. Jesus took our sins and in exchange gave us His righteousness. We get life everlasting and Jesus took our death. Here's what the Scriptures say:

Not that we are sufficiently qualified in ourselves to claim anything as coming from us, but our sufficiency and qualifications come from God. He has qualified us [making us sufficient] as ministers of a new covenant [of salvation through Christ], not of the letter [of a written code] but of the Spirit; for the letter [of the Law] kills [by revealing sin and demanding obedience], but the Spirit gives life. Now if the ministry of death, engraved in letters on stones [the covenant of the Law which led to death because of sin], came with such glory and splendor that the Israelites were not able to look steadily at the face of Moses because of its glory, [a brilliance] that was fading, how will the ministry of the Spirit [the new covenant which allows us to be Spirit-filled] fail to be even more glorious and splendid? For if the ministry that brings condemnation [the old covenant, the Law] has glory, how much more does glory overflow in the ministry that brings righteousness [the new covenant which declares believers free of guilt and sets them apart for God's special purpose]! Indeed, what had glory [the Law], in this case no longer has glory because of the glory that surpasses it [the gospel]. For if that [Law] which fades away came with glory, how much more must that [gospel] which remains and is permanent abide in glory and splendor!

2 Corinthians 3:7-11

THE DIVINE EXCHANGE

It is vitally important that we understand that when we attempt to live according to the Law, we are forsaking grace and embracing condemnation. We cannot do enough good works. As soon as we fall short, if we are not careful, guilt will creep in and our conscious will condemn us. I have repeatedly struggled in this area over the years. But the Bible clearly declares, "Therefore there is now no condemnation [no guilty verdict, no punishment] for those who are in Christ Jesus [who believe in Him as personal Lord and Savior]" (Romans 8:1).

The Law administers condemnation, but grace administers life and liberty. Condemnation is one of the biggest weapons that Satan will try to use against you, even though Jesus has already forgiven you of your sins. The spirit of condemnation will keep you from going forth in your calling because you keep replaying the tapes of your past wrongful acts. If we are not careful, the enemy will keep us from progressing and have us regressing down a slippery slope. The enemy will use sin-consciousness as a stronghold to pull us back into bondage. Why? Because when you are free, you are able to help someone else become free. "And you will know the truth [regarding salvation], and the truth will set you free [from the penalty of sin]" (John 8:32). It is by faith, and the immediate confession, that God cleanses us from all unrighteousness. This powerful process is not based on how we feel but instead on what we believe. Even if you do not feel forgiven, you are. Therefore, we must confess our sins aloud because the Law does but Faith speaks. I am the righteousness of God. For Moses writes about the righteousness, which is of the law, "The man who does those things shall live by them. But the righteousness of faith speaks" (Romans 10:5b-6a, NKJV).

We have to come to the place of recognizing it is by grace that we are saved because of the divine exchange. We give God our sins and we receive salvation through Christ. We become holy by taking on His righteousness. Jesus took all of our sicknesses, diseases, lack, and infirmities. In exchange, He gives us health, prosperity, and strength. Thank God for the great exchange that is based upon a new and better covenant. The Law submits to Grace and no longer has any dominion over us. The Law and Grace cannot co-exist because the Law makes a mockery of Grace. When we live under the Law, we are in bondage and we're miserable. All because the letter (Law) kills by revealing our sin and demanding obedience but the Spirit (Grace) produces life. Grace comes with a humble heart and a contrite spirit. It is a message of redemption and love of the Father for his children.

Grace is all about what Jesus did on our behalf. I am not required to do any works. We did not get what we deserved but Jesus got what I deserved by nailing it to the cross. "He made Christ who knew no sin to [judicially] be sin on our behalf, so that in Him we would become the righteousness of God [that is, we would be made acceptable to Him and placed in a right relationship with Him by His gracious lovingkindness]" (2 Corinthians 5:21). This is the essence of grace! He endured the hell and agony of betrayal because he knew we would never be able to be qualified to be a lamb without spot or blemish. Jesus was prepared to step out of divinity into a body of humanity. This is love!

For I am convinced [and continue to be convinced—beyond any doubt] that neither death, nor life, nor angels, nor principalities, nor things present and threatening, nor things to come, nor powers, nor height, nor depth, nor any other created thing, will be able to separate us from the [unlimited] love of God, which is in Christ Jesus our Lord.

Romans 8:38-39

God has thrown our sins into the sea of forgetfulness to remember them no more. "He shall again have compassion on us; He will subdue and tread underfoot our wickedness [destroying sin's power]" (Micah 7:19). Yes, He will cast all our sins into the depths of the sea! We have got to stop stumbling over and dredging up the things God has forgotten. As believers, we are the righteousness of God in Christ Jesus. Our righteousness is not based on our performance but on what He has already done.

Prayer of Affirmation

Thank you, God, for the divine exchange of salvation because of Jesus dying for me on the cross. You have thrown all of my sins into the sea of forgetfulness to remember them no more. I am forgiven for all of my sins—past, present, and future. I am saved through Christ. I am holy and the righteousness of God in Jesus Christ. It is because of what Christ has already done for me that I have life more abundantly here on Earth and your gift of eternal life. In Jesus' name, amen. (Colossians 2:13-14; Micah 7:19; 1 Peter 1:16, 2 Corinthians 5:21; John 10:10; Romans 6:23)

Part 3

GOD GIVES ME STRENGTH FOR EVERY STORM

I AM GIRDED WITH STRENGTH FROM GOD

For You have encircled me with strength for the battle; you have subdued under me those who rose up against me.
Psalm 18:39

Have you ever been in a situation where you felt outnumbered with no one taking your side? Or have you found yourself in the midst of a life-storm with adverse circumstances hitting from every angle like a death in the family, a car accident, a divorce, and even a lawsuit? What about when it comes to children? There can be no more profound sense of helplessness or loss than that of a parent having to confront the illness or even death of a child. Shortly after my son Aaron turned one, I found myself facing a storm when the doctor diagnosed him with asthma. How was I supposed to get through it? I didn't really know anyone who had a child with asthma, so there was no one that I could turn to for advice. I began to research the symptoms and causes of asthma on the Internet. The doctors told me that he would probably have to receive breathing treatments for a long time.

Feeling a little discouraged but not dissuaded, I remembered that I had recently ordered some books and tapes on faith and healing by Pastor Kenneth Hagin, after attending one of his healing crusades. I knew I needed to amp up my faith to believe God for a miracle, which brings us to this question, What is faith? The Bible gives this answer,

Now faith is the assurance (title deed, confirmation) of things hoped for (divinely guaranteed), and the evidence of things not seen [the conviction of their reality—faith comprehends as fact what cannot be experienced by the physical senses].
Hebrews 11:1

The James Moffat's translation reads this way, "Now faith means that we are confident of what we hope for, convinced of what we do not see." This is a faith that believes with the heart rather than believing what our physical senses may tell us. So how does faith come? According to Romans 10:17, "faith comes from hearing [what is told], and what is heard comes by the [preaching of the] message concerning Christ." So to get faith I must first hear, and what am I to hear? The preached Word of God.

Once I really caught hold to that verse, along with many other Scriptures as I listened to Pastor Hagin's messages on faith and healing over and over again, it built up my faith. I held on to Isaiah 53:5, which reads, "But He was wounded for our transgressions, He was crushed for our wickedness [our sin, our injustice, our wrongdoing]; the punishment [required] for our well-being fell on Him, and by His stripes (wounds) we are healed."

Why is the hearing of God's Word so important? It's because once you have heard a message preached, after forty-eight hours, 95 percent of what you have heard is gone. That's why on Sunday, after hearing the Word preached, you might feel invigorated and victorious and ready to weather any storm. However, by Tuesday, you seem to be headed back to being stressed, depressed, and oppressed. Why? The Word was deposited in our hearts but is then choked out by the cares of life.

Initially, I was under the authority of the doctor and following his prescribed orders; Aaron was to take medication, but it just didn't sit right with me. I know doctors can only practice medicine, but God is the healer. So I wrestled back and forth on whether to believe God for healing, or have my son on medication that was loaded with side-effects for the rest of his life. Yes, a battle pursued in the recesses of my mind. So when I began to hear the Word of God and it was planted deep in my heart, and I believed what God said about healing, I believed my son was healed in spite of the symptoms. I began confessing aloud God's Word, not the condition. I began to anoint my son with oil and pray Isaiah 53:5 over him daily. I believe God is the Great Physician, so the only way Aaron was going to be healed was for God to do it.

I had researched Albuterol (a drug used to treat Asthma) and was aware of all its side effects. Therefore, I was determined not to have my son dependent on medications for the rest of his life, or have any debilitating effects from years of taking medications. I was prompted by the Holy Spirit to go on an Esther fast of three days with no food or water, as I wanted my son to be totally healed. At one of our Friday night services, I asked the pastor to pray in agreement with me for my son's complete healing. I had faith that God had healed Aaron, so I heeded the instructions from the Holy Spirit to put away the breathing machine when I got home. I released my faith by taking action and placed the machine on the top shelf in Aaron's closet. For according to James 2:17, "So too, faith, if it does not have works [to back it up], is by itself dead [inoperative and ineffective]." James went on to say in the following verse, But someone may say, "You [claim to] have faith and I have [good] works; show me your [alleged] faith without the works [if you can], and I will show you my faith by my works [that is, by what I do]." So I switched from what the doctor prescribed to what the Word of God prescribed—a daily dose of the word of faith and prayer. I can picture it today as if it was yesterday, Aaron standing in his crib lifting his hands to the Lord with me and saying, "Thank you, Jesus, that by your stripes I am healed."

During those times following making the commitment to believe God for complete healing, Aaron experienced symptoms of asthma, and I was certainly tempted to get out the breathing machine. However, to eliminate the temptation, I returned the machine to the company. I kept my focus on listening to the tapes and rehearsing God's Word on healing. I became fully persuaded that what God promised He was well able to perform. We made the choice and kept giving thanks continually for healing until the manifestation of Aaron's healing. He was still going in for wellness check-ups and before I would go in, I prayed with conviction that no matter what the doctor would say, I was standing on the promise of God's Word. They of course wanted him to continue with taking the breathing treatments.

Over time, the symptoms grew further and further apart. God completely delivered Aaron as a child from all symptoms of asthma. God is faithful. Belief in God's promises brings about performance of what we hoped for which was total deliverance. "And blessed [spiritually fortunate and favored by God] is she who believed and confidently trusted that there would be a fulfillment of the things that were spoken to her [by the angel sent] from the Lord" (Luke 1:45). Resting on God's promise takes away any effort on our part. God's promises are for His glory to bring about victory.

Prayer of Affirmation

Thank you, Father, for girding me with strength for every battle and storm I go through in life. I know You to be faithful as my healer and deliverer. Lord, You are my rock, my fortress, and my Savior in whom I find protection. You are my shield, the power that saves me, and my place of safety. I can lean on You and rest on your promise with complete trust and belief that if You said it, then it is established. Every promise in You is "yes and amen." Your promises are for your glory to bring about victory in my life. Thank You for blessing me and bestowing favor upon me, as I believe and confidently trust that there will be a fulfillment of the things that You speak to my heart. Thank You for giving me a willing and obedient heart to follow Your instructions and to rest on Your promise until the manifestation. I refuse to back up no matter what I see or feel in the situation. I walk by faith and not by sight. I have confident expectation of good no matter how long it takes to go through each storm of life. In the storms of life, I am being made better, growing in grace, and becoming stronger in You. Thank You, Lord. I declare that it is so, in Jesus' name. Amen. (Psalm 18:39, Psalm 18:2, 2 Corinthians 1:20, 2 Corinthians 5:7)

I AM THE HEAD AND NOT THE TAIL

The LORD will make you the head (leader) and not the tail (follower); and you will be above only, and you will not be beneath, if you listen and pay attention to the commandments of the LORD your God, which I am commanding you today, to observe them carefully
Deuteronomy 28:13

Have you ever looked back on your life and began second guessing about the choices you made in the past? What if I hadn't dropped out of school? What if I didn't have a baby out of wedlock? What if I hadn't gone through with that abortion? What if I had finished college? What if I had accepted that teaching position in another state? What if I had waited to get married? What if I had pursued starting a small business? The list is endless, but the point is we have all come to a point in life where if we could turn back the hands of time and change some things, we would. We can't get stuck in yesteryear, but being retrospective can have positive outcomes.

Looking back over my life, I can see the many times when I turned left and should have turned right. I made the mistake of getting ahead of God instead of waiting on His timing and being in His perfect will. Whenever I failed to wait on God, I have been either too early or too late. I either over thought a problem because of being too anxious, or I failed to move at the right time because I feared stepping out on faith. However, I am so thankful that in the midst of it all, my Father has been patient and longsuffering with me. I understand that it is never too late to get it right and do what you should have been doing all along.

At one time, I was consistent with starting my day off early in the morning waiting on His presence until I got direction for the day. Unfortunately, somewhere along the way I stopped waiting on the Lord when I first rose in the morning, and started putting it off until I was in the car heading to work. Soon I could feel something was missing. My focus was not fully there and the cares of life were robbing me of my peace, joy, confidence, and happiness. Since then I have returned to my early morning meetings with God. By doing so, I have found myself completely satisfied in getting to know Him better. I look forward to lying in His presence with paper and pen in hand to write down my orders for the day. "Be still and know (recognize, understand) that I am God" (Psalm 46:10). As a deer pants after water brooks, so I relish my quality time with the Lord. I go into my prayer closet eager to dialogue and listen because I know that what He has to share is important for my life. I desire to spend more time in His presence knowing that everything I need is from Him. "Call to Me and I will answer you, and tell you [and even show you] great and mighty things, [things which have been confined and hidden], which you do not know and understand and cannot distinguish" (Jeremiah 33:3).

In recent years, He has taught me not to be concerned about others' opinions about me. What my utmost concern should be is what He thinks about me. That's what's important. My focus should be on getting to know Him, pleasing Him, and keeping my eyes fixed on what His Word says about me. "Am I now trying to win the favor and approval of men, or of God? Or am I seeking to please someone? If I were still trying to be popular with men, I would not be a bond-servant of Christ" (Galatians 1:10). We won't be able to go very far in achieving our goals in life if our focus is aimed on trying to please people. People are fickle. They change like the weather. However, only God remains consistent. We can put our trust in the one who remains faithful.

COME OUT, COME OUT, WHEREVER YOU ARE!

For many years, I struggled with two things. The first one was always trying to be there for others and two, being concerned about whether others liked me or not. Since I placed a lot of stock in how others felt about me, I became my own hindrance in going forth in the gifts God has given me because of fear of rejection. I also repressed what I could do because of fear of someone else being better than me. I was quick to see qualities and strengths in others, while convincing myself that I could never measure up to them. The perception of myself was skewed. I would compare myself to others and undoubtedly conclude that they were more talented. I never considered that I was equally talented with attributes, characteristics, and skill sets that made me unique. That is why it is so essential that you believe in yourself—be the best authentic you that you can be. In a society filled with so much superficiality, people want to connect with authentic individuals in whom they can relate.

Real people who are genuinely sensitive to the differences and needs of others, are hard to find but worth their weight in gold.

One of the main difficulties with relationships is that people either hide or suppress their true feelings instead of being genuine. We would rather placate people by telling them what we think they want to hear, instead of being honest. However, when we walk in God's affirmation of who He created us to be, then we will experience the liberation of who we really are. It's not about humans doing but about humans being. With faith and patience, we can become all that He has destined us to be. As God shapes us into the image of Christ, when we look into the mirror of His Word, we will start to see who God has called us to be. "So God created man in His own image, in the image and likeness of God He created him; male and female He created them" (Genesis 1:27).

Think about what happens when the sunlight passes through a magnifying glass. The sunlight gets intensified to such a degree that it causes the paper to catch fire. In a similar way, when we concentrate on the Word, it intensifies in our heart and begins to burn away everything that is not like God. Then it can bring forth the fruit of God's desire for your life. The Word becomes so powerful in our lives that it ignites every fiber of our being, and causes transformation that is pleasing to God. "But His word was in my heart like a burning fire shut up in my bones…" (Jeremiah 20:9, NKJV). Like the flaming tongues of fire that rested on the heads of those in the upper room on the day of Pentecost, the Holy Spirit today continues to light the fire of abundant life to all those who trust God.

This is how God's inspired written word comes alive and jumps off the pages by faith. It is amazing and transforming when we are so focused and believe what God says about us, that we don't accept anything different based on what people say. Don't allow what others say about you on the outside to hinder what God says about you and let it take root in your heart. Individuals will try to project their insecurities onto you to make them feel better about themselves. In many cases, the things they hate about you are what they don't like about themselves. Therefore, we have to see ourselves as He sees us by daily renewing our mind with His Word. Every morning we need to speak aloud His Word instead of speaking about the circumstance or condition. You may have an outstanding debt of $50,000. You may be living from paycheck to paycheck but recognize that this is not the end of your story. At the moment, that may happen to be your circumstance but do you believe that there will be an "after this" period in your life? Let us turn the page or adjust the mirror (open our Bible) and declare: I am the head and not the tail. I am the lender and not the borrower. "And my God will liberally supply (fill until full) your every need according to His riches in glory in Christ Jesus" (Philippians 4:19).

Prayer of Affirmation

I am adjusting my thought life by renewing my mind daily in prayer. I will rise early in the morning to seek you. As I speak to you in conversation, you will answer me and share with me great and mighty things I do not know. I will listen to get instruction in my quiet time with you. I have the mind of Christ. I believe I can have what You say I can have. I can do what You say I can do. I will go where You want me to go. I will say what You wants me to say. I call forth the Lion of the tribe of Judah within me to rise up in strength, boldness, confidence, and courage. Thank you, Lord, for making me the leader and not the follower. I will be above only and not beneath. Thank you for liberally supplying every need according to your riches in glory in Christ Jesus, in Jesus' name. Thank you. Amen. (Psalm 63:1, Jeremiah 33:3, 1 Corinthians 2:16, Deuteronomy 28:13, Philippians 4:19).

I

I AM AN IMITATOR OF GOD AS HIS CHILD

Therefore become imitators of God [copy Him and follow His example], as well-beloved children [imitate their father]; and walk continually in love [that is, value one another—practice empathy and compassion, unselfishly seeking the best for others], just as Christ also loved you and gave Himself up for us, an offering and sacrifice to God [slain for you, so that it became] a sweet fragrance.
Ephesians 5:1-2

Do you ever fill as if you don't measure up to being an example for others to follow? Do you have feelings of guilt or shame because of things you have done in the past? Do you ever think Is there any way God can use me when I don't walk the talk continually? Can you relate to having your inadequacies surface from time to time and making you just want to crawl under a rock and hide? I will admit that at times I don't see myself the way God sees me when I look at circumstances. This is why I daily have to rehearse who I am in Christ based on what His Word says and not what I see. I have to shut down the negative darts that are hurled at my mind. How do I do this? Well, I'm glad you asked.

I wake up early to begin my day with prayer and affirmation of saying what God says about my leaders, my church family, my family, myself, and others. I SHIFT my focus from seeing the negative and begin to focus on the positive. Whatever you focus upon is the very thing you begin to EMPOWER, good or bad, positive or negative. Positive confession is a powerful thing. I also begin to call those things that be not as though they were. I listen to the Bible and audio books filled with the Word and inspiration in my car while driving to and from work. I end my day by praying the Word and/or falling asleep with an audio book. I am not ignorant of Satan's devices with attacking my mind, so I have to be proactive. Now, do I do that every single day and night? Nah! I am still a work in progress as we all are striving to BE MORE, to move in a spirit of excellence. Maybe things are not as you want them to be in your family, finances, career, and relationships. You can change your perspective and call those things like you SEE it until you can see what you want to manifest, just like you called it. Doing this is preparation for me because the adage says if you fail to plan then you plan to fail. It's important to understand that this is not being religious but practical because if I don't keep Him and His words in the forefront then I have internal struggles and the circumstances of life become overwhelming. Once my focus is lost, I start spiraling out of control.

There have been periods in my life when I've been on a roller coaster ride. I needed to do something but didn't, because I was distracted by life and knocked off course. Have you been at a place where you know you should have taken a stand, but instead backed down and failed to stand up for what's right? That is when the enemy will say, 'aha' I got you to shut up. If he can get us to stop confessing, then we fall into his trap of complacency, apathy, and indecision. I have been there and do not ever want to experience that again. I have had to confront some demons in my life in order to get them to back down because the only thing they respond to is the Word of God, in the name of Jesus.

GOD OF ANOTHER CHANCE

I am so thankful that God doesn't get tired of me because of my wavering commitment to Him. As the Scriptures say in Psalm 130:3, "If God were to mark iniquity, who would stand." Jesus told His disciples that the Spirit is indeed willing but the flesh is weak (Matthew 26:41). This is why we must all press into His presence daily and early in the morning because without Him, we can do nothing. I desire to be like Him, and that means that I must follow Jesus' example. I used to feel guilty when I didn't immediately turn to Him in the midst of my challenges. I would quickly become edgy and angry. Then I would feel so disgusted with myself for taking it out on my children. My bad attitude was a reflection of being out of spiritual balance.

I know that there are many in the body of Christ who are preoccupied by their imperfections whether real or perceived. However, there is a cure for our shame, and that is to open up ourselves to reveal the secret places of our imperfections to Him. My loving Father has reassured me that there is no guilt or condemnation when I come into His presence. Growing in spiritual maturity is a process that does not happen overnight. I have to take each day one step at a time. It is not easy. I'm human, and I still struggle at times but I will continue to stay in the press until He perfects the things that concern me. "The LORD will accomplish that which concerns me; Your [unwavering] lovingkindness,

O LORD, endures forever—Do not abandon the works of Your own hands" (Psalm 138:8).

We are all a work in progress, so be encouraged daily to continue to press into His presence to get to know Him. In His presence, there is so much love, refreshment, peace, contentment, and joy. He knows our past, present, and future. There is nothing we could ever do or say that would surprise Him. Remember that shame is not about what we actually do, but it is about who we perceive ourselves to be. This is why it so essential to read and meditate on His Word to see our identity in Him. This is what He says in His Word to me: "You will show me the path of life; in Your presence is fullness of joy; in Your right hand there are pleasures forevermore" (Psalm 16:11). He desires to give us direction and strength when we spend time in His presence so that we can find rest in the path that we are taking in life. "And the LORD said, 'My presence shall go with you, and I will give you rest [by bringing you and the people into the promised land]'" (Exodus 33:14). When God's presence is with us, it brings the blessing of rest after the victory over our conflicts and confrontations has been won. We have rest from the oppression and misery we experience while traveling in the wilderness. We have rest from impending danger along the way because we know we are champions in Him. God will be with you as the greatest example in life that you have to look up to and desire as your model.

Therefore become imitators of God [copy Him and follow His example], as well-beloved children [imitate their father]; and walk continually in love [that is, value one another—practice empathy and compassion, unselfishly seeking the best for others], just as Christ also loved you and gave Himself up for us, an offering and sacrifice to God [slain for you, so that it became] a sweet fragrance.

Ephesians 5:1-2

HIS INWARD WORK PRODUCES OUTREACH

Due to the relationship we have with Jesus, we become more like Him on a daily basis. The Lord is our perfect example of reaching out to serve others because of the agape love and compassion that He had from his Father. The Scriptures declare:

We are all called as believers to show love one to another within the household of faith. Let the peace of Christ [the inner calm of one who walks daily with Him] be the controlling factor in your hearts [deciding and settling questions that arise]. To this peace indeed you were called as members in one body [of believers]. And be thankful [to God always]. Let the [spoken] word of Christ have its home within you [dwelling in your heart and mind—permeating every aspect of your being] as you teach [spiritual things] and admonish and train one another with all wisdom, singing psalms and hymns and spiritual songs with thankfulness in your hearts to God. Whatever you do [no matter what it is] in word or deed, do everything in the name of the Lord Jesus [and in dependence on Him], giving thanks to God the Father through Him.

Colossians 3:15-17

During Jesus' earthly ministry, everywhere He went He fulfilled the will of the Father as He ministered to the needs of others. Imitating His example, our outreach is to our family and others. We are to bless, encourage, comfort, and speak well of others, and we are to speak truthful and admonishing words, be hospitable and giving to one another. Let me share a golden nugget with you. I have found that whenever I take the focus off my circumstances and help someone else that is going through, there is no way I can stay upset, depressed, or in the pit. The word is true: "The generous man [is a source of blessing and] shall be prosperous and enriched, and he who waters will himself be watered [reaping the generosity he has sown]" (Proverbs 11:25). It works every time. Whenever your focus shifts from self to sow into someone else, the same will boomerang back into your life. As my mom likes to say, "You can't touch a rose without getting some of that fragrance back on you."

Prayer of Affirmation

Lord, help me to remember that my identity is in You. I imitate You and follow Your example as a beloved child. I will walk continually in love and demonstrate love by unselfishly seeking the best for others, even when I need to sacrifice my time and resources to do so. When I struggle or am overtaken by guilt or shame, please help me to remember your words: "It is finished." Thank You for your Son being offered as a sacrifice for all my sins, including my guilt and shame, on the cross. Thank You for showing me the path of life as I press to get into Your presence to experience fullness of joy and pleasures forevermore. Your presence shall go with me as I journey through the wilderness. And I am at rest as You bring me safely into the promise land, in Jesus' name. Thank You. Amen. (Ephesians 5:1-2, Psalm 16:11, Exodus 33:14).

I AM JUSTIFIED BY FAITH

Therefore, since we have been justified [that is, acquitted of sin, declared blameless before God] by faith, [let us grasp the fact that] we have peace with God [and the joy of reconciliation with Him] through our Lord Jesus Christ (the Messiah, the Anointed). Through Him we also have access by faith into this [remarkable state of] grace in which we [firmly and safely and securely] stand. Let us rejoice in our [a]hope and the confident assurance of [experiencing and enjoying] the glory of [our great] God [the manifestation of His excellence and power]. And not only this, but [with joy] let us exult in our sufferings and rejoice in our hardships, knowing that hardship (distress, pressure, trouble) produces patient endurance; and endurance, proven character (spiritual maturity); and proven character, hope and confident assurance [of eternal salvation]. Such hope [in God's promises] never disappoints us, because God's love has been abundantly poured out within our hearts through the Holy Spirit who was given to us.
Romans 5:1-5

Have you ever gone through a challenging time wondering if it would ever end? Are you experiencing pressure or trouble in your life as you are reading this book right now? Can you identify with the Scripture above that commands you to rejoice in your hardship knowing that it will produce patient endurance, proven character, hope, and confident assurance of eternal salvation? God's intent is for us to move from being justified (forgiven of all our sins) to being sanctified (set apart, growing in spiritual maturity, and holiness), and move to glorification (being fit for the master's use to bring Him glory in the earth). All that we have gone through is not by happenstance but has been a set up to do a deeper work from the inside out. We definitely go through some transformations by the fiery tests and trials that we have in life. Sometimes during the battle, we are kicking and screaming all the way through, preoccupied with the problem. At other times, it is with calmness and patience, with our focus on Him. The route we take, problem-focused or Christ-focused, will determine whether we will experience more wilderness or greater wonder. It's not easy to keep your focus on the promise when you are surrounded by doubt. Doubt can come in many forms: debt, living from paycheck to paycheck, or being on the cusp of unemployment. Yet with as many tests that I have experienced, God has brought me out of each one of them victoriously. I know Him to be a promise keeper. Each time God has prepared a promotion for me at my place of employment. He would always trouble the waters making things at work uncomfortable.

Typically, my hours would be reduced due to a drop in patient census, and it would push me to seek Him to find out what to do or where to go next. I can sense when a door is about to shut, and that's why I am currently starting a part-time online business for health and nutrition. I am taking a leap of faith as it as has been a dream of mine for some years to work from home. God has me in a place where I am totally dependent on Him. Thus, it isn't always a comfortable place to be, but it's a good place to be. I know that I can do all things through Christ who strengthens me, but I am relying on the leading of the Holy Spirit to guide my steps.

Starting a new business is new territory for me, but I am moving on a word the Lord spoke to my heart to reach out to promote health and wellness in the marketplace online. I reached out and reconnected with my sister-friend Sandi Krakowski, who is a direct response marketer and copywriter for small-business owners online. I followed her lead for tips and tools on how to reach out to individuals to add value, inspiration, and encouragement via social media. She is an answer to prayer because, God often guides and blesses you through others.

MY BOAZ BLESSING ARRIVES

Once I began to share health and wellness tips, recipes, and inspiration daily on social media, I began to build a community of friends. I looked forward to the daily dialogue and relationships that were developing over the course of time. I waited patiently for the next step because I really wanted to be accountable in a group setting where I coached people who were ready to have a turnaround in their health through natural alternatives. Sunday, October 11, 2015, I received my answer. I had just finished praying in my basement and went upstairs to get into the shower when I heard the Holy Spirit tell me to reach out to a certain person as a coach in my niche for operating my business online. (How many of you get instructions and solutions to your prayers while in the bathroom?) I had been following Rochelle Griffin's business page for a little over a year because she was a coach for health, nutrition, business, and personal growth. So without thinking about it, I went to her Facebook page and looked on her website to send her a message about connecting with her to be my mentor. One day, I would like to mentor clients and other coaches via social media too. After dialoguing back and forth, it felt like it would was a good fit. It was like a dream come true. I also had a tough decision to make because it would involve switching companies. However, with research, I saw that this would be a far better program for my health, the health of those that I would in turn mentor, and one day soon be able to retire from my job.

Friday morning, October 16, 2015, I said to God, I need to hear from you that I am making the right choice. Holy Spirit answered and said, *"I am doing a new thing. It shall spring forth. I am making a way for you to come out of your desert place. All that you put your hands to do shall prosper. Now is the set time. Be courageous. Follow My lead."* I looked up the passage of Scripture on my Bible app and began to weep in His presence and said, "Thank you, Father." *"Listen carefully, I am about to do a new thing, NOW it will spring forth; will you not be aware of it? I will even put a road in the wilderness, rivers in the desert"* (Isaiah 43:19).

Later that morning I told her I was ready to get started. She went on to state, "I consider it divine intervention that you contacted me when you did. You had no clue I was opening my mentorship the next day!" Wow, this was a confirmation. I contacted her on Sunday, and she released the mentorship program on her Facebook page Monday, October 12, 2015. I will be getting direct expert advice and assistance with step-by-step action to in turn do the same for those whom I will mentor and coach online. I view my mentor as a Boaz blessing because she is a working believer that God is using to be His agent of blessing to me.

My prayer for the last few months has been to let someone connect with me and invest in me so that as I am supernaturally blessed, I in turn, can be a blessing to someone else in their health and finances. Let my status change in 24 hours. Yes, this is pretty radical, but this is the type of prayer that my spiritual dad encouraged us to pray this year. I have big dreams that I desire to see God fulfill in the life of my family and His people. Once again I was learning the importance of stepping out on faith and following the Holy Spirit's lead. Often our miracle breakthrough comes first with following a set of instructions that will take us outside of our comfort zone.

So with the expectation I see that breakthrough is going to happen for many to experience health and wellness along with financial freedom.

I do believe I am going to have another great testimony to share with you either at the completion of this book or in the next one to come.

Prayer of Affirmation

I will listen carefully to your instructions and trust Your leading even when it does not make sense. I will boldly step out in faith so that I can please you, Father. Help me to recognize that when you shut doors, it is because you have opened a brand new door that is greater. The doors You shut no man can open and the doors that You have open for me, no man can close. You are doing a new thing. It shall spring forth. You are making a way for me to come out of my desert place. Right now in my desert places, you are allowing rivers to flow. My diligence will pay off. All that I put my hands to do (work) shall prosper. Now is the set time for You to favor me. I am courageous. I am confident. I choose to drop my reins and my control to follow Your lead always.
(Hebrews 11:6, Revelation 3:8, Isaiah 43:19, Psalm 102:13, Proverbs 12:24)

I AM KEPT BY THE POWER OF GOD

*Who are kept by the power of God through faith for salvation
ready to be revealed in the last time.*
1 Peter 1:5, NKJV

How many of you truly know that if it was not for God's supernatural protection you probably wouldn't be here right now? Have you been late leaving for work only to find out that you just missed an accident by moments? Have you had an intuition to go to a meeting, a conference, an individual, or a worship service and that became your greatest blessing or breakthrough? All I can tell you is that God does indeed work in mysterious ways. And I have had numerous occasions to know that I am one hundred percent without a shadow of doubt kept by the power of God.

HE IS A MIRACLE WORKER

I was driving home from work one day and normally make a left at the light on Rotunda to get on the Southfield Freeway to pick up I-94 West to head home. As I approached the light, it turned green. I heard in my spirit "keep straight." So I kept straight on Rotunda but thought it odd as I only went that way when I needed gas. I kept straight on Rotunda and made a left on Pelham. Just as I came to the gas station at Pelham and Vanborn, the traffic light was red. I came to a stop and when it turned green, my car started to drag as I applied the gas. I was sputtering, and moving very slowly. I barely made it through the light and pulled into the Marathon station at a gas pump and my car cut OFF! I started it up and the radio came on. Heat shot out through the vents, and the red battery light was flashing. The same thing happened when I tried to start it up again to move the car off to the side of the gas station.

I made a call for road service, and when the tow-truck driver arrived, he took me to the Amoco service station. They tested everything under the hood, gave the battery some juice, and really couldn't find anything wrong other than I would eventually need a new battery since I still had the original. God is so AMAZING! Well I wasn't going to leave without first getting a new battery. As my mom said, "We don't even want to think about what could have happened if I had taken the expressway." God is always looking out for our protection, and I do believe those angels helped me to get my car to a safe place. I truly thank God for giving me direction that day, and most importantly that I followed His leading. Yep, I heard that other voice say just now, "Well, you miss it more than you follow through because you over think things before you make a move." Shut up, devil! I am a work in progress, and God gives me another chance to make the right move.

Prayer of Affirmation

Father, thank you for keeping me by your mighty power. Thank you for surrounding me with angels—both seen and unseen—that protect me from hurt, harm, and danger. Thank you for keeping me from all evil and for keeping my life. Thank you for keeping my going out and my coming in from this time forth and forevermore. Though the weapons may be formed against me they will not prosper. I am thankful for Your continual protection over my life. I praise You for all the times for what could have happened but didn't because of the swiftness of Your grace. Thank you, in Jesus' name. Amen. (Psalm 46:1, Luke 4:10, Psalm 121:7-8, Isaiah 54:17)

I AM LOVED BY GOD WITH AN EVERLASTING LOVE

The LORD appeared to me (Israel) from ages past, saying, "I have loved you with an everlasting love; Therefore with lovingkindness I have drawn you and continued My faithfulness to you.
Jeremiah 31:3

GOD'S LOVE IS UNCONDITIONAL

Some years ago, I had to come to the realization that I can never earn the Father's love by being good enough. He loves me with an everlasting and unconditional love. That means even before I was born God loved me. Before I ever came to know who He was after I was birthed, God loved me. The love He has for you and me is unwavering and unconditional. It is established in His promise that He will never ever stop loving us. The LORD appeared to me (Israel) from ages past, saying, "I have loved you with an everlasting love; Therefore with lovingkindness I have drawn you and continued My faithfulness to you" (Jeremiah 31:3).

LOVE YOURSELF, LOVE OTHERS

Love yourself and continue to love your family to life day-by-day, and watch God change your heart. He will fill each compartment of your heart with His love. Have an expectation that circumstances in your life will shift for the better. One of the audio books I listen to often is The Power of Right Believing by Joseph Prince. We have to believe right before we can ever experience the truth of what the Word says. It is not just about talking out the truth. It is taking a firm stand on believing that truth first. Above and beyond what circumstances may present, it is refusing to back down. Experiencing pain, sorrow, disappointment, and problems in life in no way diminishes God's love for us. His Word informs us that "Man, who is born of a woman, is short-lived and full of turmoil" (Job 14:1). Therefore, we are going to have days when we are having high mountain-top experiences and days when we sink down low to the valley. It is in the valley where we are put to the test to remain faithful in our praise, worship, and thanksgiving to God the same as we did when life was going well.

No matter what position or station in life we find ourselves, God's love remains constant toward us. As the Bible declares, even when we were enemies, Christ died for us. So it doesn't matter whether we are on cloud nine or in a pit of despair, God's love remains. This remains true even when we step outside of His will and fall into rebellion, stubbornness, or lust. I've done it on many occasions when my affections were divided over other things and not fully allowing my heart's compartments to be satisfied with Him. And it is when I began to chase after and thirst after Him that He gives me so much joy and peace. I am learning more and more to be a God chaser with a yearning for more of Him to fill me. "As the deer pants [longingly] for the water brooks, So my soul pants [longingly] for You, O God. My soul (my life, my inner self) thirsts for God, for the living God" (Psalm 42:1-2).

We can rest assured the Father absolutely loves us and wants what is best for His children. What is best for us can only be found in His perfect will. How is it that we can find His perfect will? It is through spending time alone with Him in prayer and meditation, and studying His Word. When you do that, in return, He will nourish, guide, reveal, and give you specific instructions for your life. "Call to Me and I will answer you, and tell you [and even show you] great and mighty things, [things which have been confined and hidden], which you do not know and understand and cannot distinguish" (Jeremiah 33:3). He wants to share His plan with us. Therefore, He gently knocks at the door of our heart and desires that we would welcome Him in. When you invite the Lord in, He will then reveal things to you about your life that separate you from Him, things you would never realize without His revelation. He will give you direction and order your steps in the way you should go. "For I am convinced [and continue to be convinced—beyond any doubt] that neither death, nor life, nor angels, nor principalities, nor things present and threatening, nor things to come, nor powers, nor height, nor depth, nor any other created thing, will be able to separate us from the [unlimited] love of God, which is in Christ Jesus our Lord" (Romans 8:38-39). Who wouldn't serve a God like that? Our Father sending his only son to die on the cross to cover all of our sins past, present, and future. That's love! There have been numerous times over the years when I have made mistakes, rebelled, been stubborn, and had to repent of my ways. Yet each time, He has been graceful by giving me what I do not deserve. He also has given me mercy with not giving me what I do deserve. His love surpasses comprehension and comparison. I know that my natural and spiritual parents are there for me, but as mere people, they are limited in what they can do. Our heavenly Father surpasses all human effort, capability, and love.

Through His grace and love for us, He has given each of us a gift that is to be used to further His kingdom. Then on top of that, He gives us eternal rewards for being good and faithful servants. He could have simply left us to our muck and mire, but instead He found us, saved us, cleaned us up, empowered us to serve Him and then blesses us with eternal life. God is faithful! Can you think of the many times He delivered you out of strongholds, sickness, accidents, and bondage? You were headed for destruction but because of his divine protection, you have life more abundantly. You should have lost your mind, but you are still standing and in your right mind. I'm still standing and praising God. He has kept me. That's love.

Prayer of Affirmation

Father, I thank You for giving me what I don't even deserve (grace) and not giving me what I do deserve (mercy). I yearn for more and more of You in my life every day just as the deer pants after the water. Daily my soul thirsts for the living God. Fill me up, God, to overflow. Fill me with more of Your love so that I can love others as You love me. I seek You early in the morning so that you can give me guidance and direction for my day. I seek you to answer my questions because you said to call on You and You would share with me great and mighty things that have been hidden which I do not know and understand. I am convinced [and continue to be convinced—beyond any doubt] that neither death, nor life, nor angels, nor principalities, nor things present and threatening, nor things to come, nor powers, nor height, nor depth, nor any other created thing, will be able to separate me from the [unlimited] love of God, which is in Christ Jesus our Lord. Thank you for your loving kindness and faithfulness that you continually show towards me. I love you, Father. I love you, Holy Spirit. I love you, Lord. In Jesus' name, amen. (Psalm 42:1-2, Psalm 63:1, Jeremiah 33:3, Romans 8:38-39, Jeremiah 31:3)

I AM MORE THAN A CONQUEROR

Yet in all these things we are more than conquerors and gain an overwhelming victory through Him who loved us [so much that He died for us].
Romans 8:37

HERE WE GO AGAIN

Have you ever been in a situation where an individual has tried to manipulate you or back you into a corner to impose their will upon you? Has anyone on your job ever pressured you to do something you didn't want to do, like forced overtime? Have you ever had to take a stand even though it could cost you a position, ministry, or title? Last year I took a stand by not being forced to get a flu vaccination. I instead chose to wear a mask. Wearing the mask is based on the premise that whoever wears a mask, prevents that individual from spreading any contagious virus. However, when individuals asked me why I was wearing the mask, I retorted, "So I don't get exposed to the flu or colds while working here." My co-worker thought I was crazy. Ironically, some of those who took the flu shot still ended up getting the flu. Then came the news report that the wrong batch was given. Then on November 5, 2015, they now want to make the flu shot mandatory where you have to have a medical or religious reason for exemption.

THIS IS A GOLIATH

You mean to tell me that if I refuse to get the flu shot I have to have a medical or religious reason or I will be fired from my job. The devil is a lie! I saw this as just being an intimidating Goliath.

Then David said to the Philistine, "You come to me with a sword, a spear, and a javelin, but I come to you in the name of the LORD of hosts, the God of the armies of Israel, whom you have taunted. This day the LORD will hand you over to me, and I will strike you down and cut off your head. And I will give the corpses of the army of the Philistines this day to the birds of the sky and the wild beasts of the earth, so that all the earth may know that there is a God in Israel, and that this entire assembly may know that the LORD does not save with the sword or with the spear; for the battle is the LORD'S and He will hand you over to us."

1 Samuel 17:45-47

The whole controversy over the mandatory flu shots grabbed headlines across the nation. Many felt the same way about being forced to take shots that they didn't want to take. Yes, it would have been simpler to take the shot. So why wouldn't I get it? Because it is my choice not theirs. I have the freedom and the constitutional right to choose what to put into my body. Additionally, I believe that my God will back me up. Who are these health care giants that are coming at me with intimidation, anyway?

I had a doctor's appointment November 5, 2015 and had my physician to sign a medical exemption form of my refusal for the vaccine as "religious reasons." I also submitted a document that stated I was exercising my rights under the:

First Amendment of the U.S. Constitution and Title VII of the Civil Rights Act of 1964 as amended Nov. 1, 1980; Part 1605. 1-Guidelines on Discrimination Because of Religion to receive Religious Exemption from Vaccination and got a notary public seal.

We have to do our due diligence and not just conform to the status quo. Our silence on various issues will have a rippling effect. If it does not affect us now, it could be detrimental in years and generations to come. What did Paul say to do after having done all that we know how to do?

Therefore, put on the complete armor of God, so that you will be able to [successfully] resist and stand your ground in the evil day [of danger], and having done everything [that the crisis demands], to stand firm [in your place, fully prepared, immovable, victorious]. So stand firm and hold your ground, HAVING TIGHTENED THE WIDE BAND OF TRUTH (personal integrity, moral courage) AROUND YOUR WAIST and HAVING PUT ON THE BREASTPLATE OF RIGHTEOUSNESS (an upright heart).

Ephesians 6:13-14

I did all I could do, so now I am just going to STAND. Though the enemy will construct weapons to attack us, God says no weapon formed against His people will not prosper. I am standing on this promise as I submitted my forms on Monday, November 9, 2015. I was exempted from taking the mandatory flu shot. *"No weapon that is formed against you will succeed; and every tongue that rises against you in judgment you will condemn. This [peace, righteousness, security, and triumph over opposition] is the heritage of the servants of the LORD, and this is their vindication from Me,"* says the LORD (Isaiah 54:17).

On December 21, 2015, I was a handed a letter from the human resource department. It stated that based on the information provided in my request citing my strongly held religious beliefs that do not permit me to receive the influenza vaccine, I was EXEMPT from taking the 2015-2016 influenza vaccine. After reading that, I gave God the glory. My Father is awesome and faithful, my strong deliverer. I was so thankful.

Prayer of Affirmation

Father, my hope and trust are in you for protection against my enemies. Let the oppressor be broken in pieces. Though I may be facing mountains of debt, lack, poverty, joblessness, homelessness, sickness, and experiencing a relationship tug-of-war, I speak to every mountain in my life (insert each by name) and command them to be removed and cast into the sea, in the name of Jesus. Every mountain in my way will become a plain. No weapon that is formed against me will succeed; and every tongue that rises against me in judgment I will condemn. This [peace, righteousness, security, and triumph over opposition] is the heritage of the servants of the LORD, and this is my vindication from You. Having done all that I know to do, I will stand and rest on your promise. Thank you, in Jesus name. Amen. (Psalm 72:4, Mark 11:23, Zechariah 4:7, Ephesians 6:13-14, Isaiah 54:17)

Rest

Part 4

WILLING TO CONFRONT AND CONQUER MY ENEMY

I AM NEVER ALONE FOR HE'LL NEVER LEAVE ME NOR FORSAKE ME

Be strong and courageous, do not be afraid or tremble in dread before them, for it is the LORD your God who goes with you. He will not fail you or abandon you.
Deuteronomy 31:6

Have you ever been surrounded by people, yet still feel all alone? Have you ever been between a rock and a hard place, needing help but not knowing where to find it? Have you ever taken a stand for what is right and you're in the minority? Such was the case of the three Hebrew boys Shadrach, Meshach, and Abed-nego. They were alone in their refusal to bow down and worship King Nebuchadnezzar's golden image.

Then Nebuchadnezzar in a furious rage gave a command to bring Shadrach, Meshach, and Abed-nego; and these men were brought before the king. Nebuchadnezzar said to them, "Is it true, Shadrach, Meshach, and Abed-nego, that you do not serve my gods or worship the golden image which I have set up? Now if you are ready, when you hear the sound of the horn, pipe, lyre, trigon, harp, dulcimer, and all kinds of music, to fall down and worship the image which I have made, very good. But if you do not worship, you shall be thrown at once into the midst of a furnace of blazing fire; and what god is there who can rescue you out of my hands?" Shadrach, Meshach, and Abed-nego answered the king, "O Nebuchadnezzar, we do not need to answer you on this point. If it be so, our God whom we serve is able to rescue us from the furnace of blazing fire, and He will rescue us from your hand, O king. But even if He does not, let it be known to you, O king, that we are not going to serve your gods or worship the golden image that you have set up!"

Daniel 3:13-18

In this passage, we see that Shadrach, Meshach, and Abed-nego refused to bow down to worship anything or anyone besides the living God. As a result of their stance for the living God, they were thrown into the fiery furnace. I'm sure people ridiculed and talked about them. Can you imagine being in a situation where you are not taking a stand against your family member or friend but you are standing face-to-face with a powerful king? It appears that you are in the minority and have to face a fiery trial all alone with pressure, ridicule, and being ostracized by others. Consider the strength and courage of the young men who were so persuaded by the sovereignty and power of their God, that they told King Nebuchadnezzar that the God whom they served was able to rescue them. And even if God did not, they were still not going to serve the king's gods or worship the golden image. "Beloved, do not be surprised at the fiery ordeal which is taking place to test you [that is, to test the quality of your faith], as though something strange or unusual were happening to you" (1 Peter 4:12).

They had such an unshakable faith to know that God would be their deliverer because He is always with them. "What then shall we say to all these things? If God is for us, who can be [successful] against us?" (Romans 8:31). They were not alone in facing their fiery trial. Be encouraged to know that know no matter what you are facing right now, your strength is not in yourself or in other people. You are not alone. Jesus is right there in the fire with you.

But He has said to me, "My grace is sufficient for you [My lovingkindness and My mercy are more than enough—always available—regardless of the situation]; for [My] power is being perfected [and is completed and shows itself most effectively] in [your] weakness." Therefore, I will all the more gladly boast in my weaknesses, so that the power of Christ [may completely enfold me and] may dwell in me.

2 Corinthians 12:9

I believe that when the three Hebrew boys made their boast in God, He stepped in and showed Himself as Almighty. Our strength is made perfect in our weakness because of our dependence upon Him when the heat turns up in our lives. No matter what we are going through, His Word commands us to be strong. "Be strong and courageous, do not be afraid or tremble in dread before them, for it is the LORD your God who goes with you. He will not fail you or abandon you" (Deuteronomy 31:6).

As you continue to stand on His truth and not look at the situation—no matter how daunting it may be—watch how God will show up!

Then Nebuchadnezzar the king [looked and] was astounded, and he jumped up and said to his counselors, "Did we not throw three men who were tied up into the midst of the fire?" They replied to the king, "Certainly, O king." He answered, "Look! I see four men untied, walking around in the midst of the fire, and they are not hurt! And the appearance of the fourth is like a son of the gods!" Then Nebuchadnezzar approached the door of the blazing furnace and said, "Shadrach, Meshach, and Abed-nego, servants of the Most High God, come out [of there]! Come here!" Then Shadrach, Meshach, and Abed-nego came out of the midst of the fire. The satraps, the prefects, the governors and the king's counselors gathered around them and saw that in regard to these men the fire had no effect on their bodies—their hair was not singed, their clothes were not scorched or damaged, even the smell of smoke was not on them.
Daniel 3:24-27

The king was astounded to see four men in the fire and recognized that one looked to be the appearance of "a son of the gods!" The New King James Version reads "like the Son of God." Do you see how God will show up right there in the fire with you. The men were bound going into the situation. Yet they came out of the fire untied and with no effect on their bodies, hair, or clothes. They took a stand for whom they trusted and believed. We can rest on His promises that when we take a stand for God and having done all we continue to stand, we shall never be alone. He is faithful to bring us through the fiery trials of life victoriously. "Therefore, put on the complete armor of God, so that you will be able to [successfully] resist and stand your ground in the evil day [of danger], and having done everything [that the crisis demands], to stand firm [in your place, fully prepared, immovable, victorious]." (Ephesians 6:13)

Prayer of Affirmation
Thank You, Father, that I am never alone in my fiery trials of life. I am not surprised at this fiery trial I am going through. It is just testing the quality of my faith. Where I am weak I count on Your strength to show up powerfully in my life. I am strong and courageous because it is you, my God, who goes with me. You will never fail me

nor abandon me. In all the things I face of various conflicts, persecution, ridicule, and accusation I know that You cause me to always to triumph. If You are for me, then who can be against me? I will stand with Your complete armor, so that I will be able to successfully resist and stand my ground when facing the hottest trial of my life. And having done all that I know to do in my crisis, I will stand firm, fully prepared, immovable, and victorious. In Jesus' name, amen. (2 Corinthians 12:1, I Peter 4:12, Deuteronomy 31:6, 2 Corinthians 2:14, Romans 8:31, Ephesians 6:13)

I AM AN OVERCOMER

Yet in all these things we are more than conquerors and gain an overwhelming victory through Him who loved us [so much that He died for us]. For I am convinced [and continue to be convinced—beyond any doubt] that neither death, nor life, nor angels, nor principalities, nor things present and threatening, nor things to come, nor powers, nor height, nor depth, nor any other created thing, will be able to separate us from the [unlimited] love of God, which is in Christ Jesus our Lord.
Romans 8:37-39

Have you been in a situation where you keep procrastinating and trying to avoid a conflict instead of dealing with the problem? What's really going on? Is it because you are dealing with some fear about the situation? Is it because you are afraid of the unknown and uncertain about the possible changes that could come about? Well take comfort in the message of the Scriptures concerning King Saul and David. David must have been experiencing overwhelming fear, stress, and pain while on the run from Saul. It is one thing to deal with attitudes and negatives words coming against you, but how do you confront someone who is on a mission to kill you! "Now Saul told his son Jonathan and all his servants to kill David, but Jonathan, Saul's son, greatly delighted in David" (1 Samuel 19:1).

At some point in our lives, we have to confront various types of giants. They may not have been physical giants such as was Goliath, but these situational giants can be just as foreboding. They may have been giants in your home, on your job, within ministry, or in other relationships. In 1 Samuel 19, David has to flee from his father-in-law, King Saul, who was out to kill him. Forced to live on the run, by happenstance, an opportunity presented itself for David to get even. While Saul was out searching for David, he went into a cave to relieve himself—in the very cave where David was hiding. Saul was unaware that David was there and watching him. While Saul was indisposed, David could have easily killed him. Instead, David had mercy upon him and spared his life. When David's men asked him why he didn't act on an opportune time to kill his enemy, here is what David said, "The LORD forbid that

I should do this thing to my master, the LORD'S anointed, to put out my hand against him, since he is the anointed of the LORD" (1 Samuel 24:6).

The sole reason David would not lift a hand against Saul was because Saul was the Lord's anointed. At that pivotal point he confronts Saul. Then David also got up afterward and went out of the cave and called after Saul, saying,

"My lord the king!" And when Saul looked behind him, David bowed with his face to the ground and lay himself face down. David said to Saul, "Why do you listen to the words of men who say, 'David seeks to harm you?' Behold, your eyes have seen today how the LORD had given you into my hand in the cave. Some told me to kill you, but I spared you; I said, 'I will not reach out my hand against my lord, for he is the LORD'S anointed.' Look, my father! Indeed, see the hem of your robe in my hand! Since I cut off the hem of your robe and did not kill you, know and understand [without question] that there is no evil or treason in my hands. I have not sinned against you, though you are lying in wait to take my life. May the LORD judge between me and you; and may the LORD avenge me on you; but my hand shall not be against you. As the proverb of the ancients says, 'Out of the wicked comes wickedness'; but my hand shall not be against you. After whom has the king of Israel come out? Whom do you pursue [with three thousand men]? A dead dog, a single flea? May the LORD be the judge and render judgment between me and you; and may He see and plead my cause and vindicate me by saving me from your hand."

1 Samuel 24: 8-15

It is easy to yield to passion. It is gratifying to get even especially when someone's out to get you. However, when we take matters into our own hands, we often fall into the same trap that our enemy set for us. Often, the key to victory is knowing whether to confront or disengage. Like David, you have to be willing to yield your wrath to God, so you will not end up in bondage by seeking revenge. Besides, the Bible teaches that, "For man's anger does not promote the righteousness God [wishes and requires]" (James 12:20).

STOP RUNNING FROM CONFRONTATION

It is amazing what happens when we stop running away and deal with confrontation and struggles head on. There is no reason to rehearse what to say because God will give us what to say at the right time.

When David had finished saying these words to Saul, Saul said, "Is this your voice, my son David?" Then Saul raised his voice and wept. He said to David, "You are more righteous and upright [in God's eyes] than I; for you have done good to me, but I have done evil to you. You have declared today the good that you have done to me, for when the LORD put me into your hand, you did not kill me. For if a man finds his enemy, will he let him go away unharmed? So may the LORD reward you with good in return for what you have done for me this day. Now, behold, I know that you will certainly be king and that the kingdom of Israel will be established in your hand. So now swear to me by the LORD that you will not cut off my descendants after me and that you will not destroy my name from my father's household (extended family)." David gave Saul his oath; and Saul went home, but David and his men went up to the mountain stronghold.

1 Samuel 24:16-22

Wow, David's mercy had a powerful impact on Saul—it brought Saul to tears. Since David did the right thing in God's eyes, King Saul vowed to not continue pursuing him. In return, Saul asked David to swear an oath not to destroy his descendants, as was customary when an opposing king succeeded another. This oath David kept later when he showed bountiful grace and mercy to one of Saul's descendants lame in both feet, named Mephibosheth (2 Samuel 9:13).

BACK TO ME

All the stress and anxiety began to take a toll on me physically. All this was happening in January 1995, the year that I had my oldest son, Aaron. However, by June 1996, I was still carrying excess weight from my pregnancy. I could no longer give the excuse of it being "baby fat." I was feeling the effects of being overweight, tired and sluggish. Whenever I had to chase after Aaron, I would quickly become winded and have to sit down. The revelation that I had to do something about my health came when I was attending our Total Woman Ministry's class taught by Frances McMullan. Yes, the struggle was real! I could choose to change my life or remain unhealthy and overweight.

It was like riding a roller coaster, going up and down not only on the scale, but in life. Attending the Total Woman Ministry class taught me that I was not in this boat alone. At times I got so fed up with the challenges on my job and in my relationships that I just wanted it to be over! Kaput! Done! I know that I created some of those problems, but that fact didn't stop me from wishing I could wave a magic wand to make all the extra pounds disappear. I was so deep in denial that I was wearing skirts with elastic waists bands, sweatshirts, and sweatpants. I refused to face the fact that I could no longer where a size twelve. I remember being upset because I thought I could walk into Casual Corner and put on anything. However, that was merely wishful thinking. I had outgrown Casual Corner and had to shop at Lane Bryant, the store that specializes in plus sizes.

I had talked myself into being content that I could find my clothes in a stylish larger size, but who was I kidding? I had to come to grips with the fact that it wasn't about the size of the clothes; it was really the battle of my mind and the internal issues I wasn't willing to face. After being in denial long enough, I was tired of kidding myself. Enough was enough. So I swallowed my pride and asked my sisters in the group if they could help me find a solution. One of my sisters in the ministry recommended I read the book Help Lord…The Devil Wants Me Fat. That book, along with many others, started me on a journey of prayer and fasting. For the type of strongholds that had a grip on me, I knew could not be broken by prayer alone. As the Word teaches us about removing certain strongholds in our lives, "howbeit this kind goeth not out but by prayer and fasting (Matthew 17:21, KJV).

I realized that food had become my way of coping. Rather than turn to the Lord, I found comfort in foods like burgers and fries and sweets. God wanted to have all of my heart, and I had to rid myself of an idol (food) that was taking His place. As I talked with Him more about my issues, meditating on His Word, and stopped pacifying my flesh with comfort foods, the strongholds were broken and the pounds fell off. Was it easy? No! After reading Help Lord…The Devil Wants Me Fat, I was determined because there were many benefits to being healthy. I wanted to be successful in my weight-loss efforts, but the enemy wanted me to remain where I was—discouraged, discontent, disappointed, and dissatisfied.

The temptation was relentless. The devil would always say, "Go ahead and eat. No one's looking." And wouldn't you know it, after making up my mind to fast and pray, my co-workers decide to bring in free donuts and bagels. So staying delivered was a tug-of-war between my flesh and my will, and I knew I couldn't win the battle in my own strength. I wanted God to superimpose His will over mine. His grace supernaturally gave me strength to resist sweet temptations like chocolate, salty chips, and mint chocolate ice cream. I immediately would use my sword of the Spirit (which is the Word of God) and talk back to the enemy—aloud—confessing these three Scripture inspired affirmations:

My body is the temple of the Holy Spirit and I am not hungry.
I do not live by bread only but by every word that proceeds out of the mouth of God.
Father I esteem the words of your mouth more so than my necessary food.

Not only did I recite them at work, but I also recited them at home while standing in front of my refrigerator. I had index cards with the Scriptures taped to the fridge always there to remind me. As I became more determined, it became easier around the third day of the fast. I made it through my first ten-day fast, from June 20 to July 1, 1996. Eventually, the stronghold of gluttony was pulled down, and I re-gained my physical energy and strength. Spiritually, I was also victorious because during that time I received the baptism of the Holy Spirit with the evidence of speaking in tongues while sitting in my living room.

Since I have been on this road, at times I still waver with overindulging in the sweets on my birthday and during special events. And in moments of weakness, there have been times when I have made unhealthy choices. Remember, I told you that I am not perfect but I serve an awesome and perfect God. As a good compromise, once a week I make it a choice to have a "treat" meal but I don't turn it into a cheat week like I used to back in the day. I don't want to take that downward spiral again but desire to be an example so that I can help others with their health and nutrition. Having had the roller-coaster effect in this area over the years, I can so relate to others who are experiencing a stronghold in that area. It is my strong desire to help others find a healthy lifestyle of nutrition and fitness through my Mind Shape Up community on Facebook. The fight and struggle is real, but I know that God is well able to help us conquer those things in life that we are willing to confront. "Yet in all these things we are more than conquerors and gain an overwhelming victory through Him who loved us [so much that He died for us]" (Romans 8:37).

My struggle happens to be food that I use in an attempt to satisfy my hungry soul. But we all have something we may turn to as an addictive behavior, such as drugs, alcohol, shopping, attention seeking, sex, all in place of the One who can fill our deepest longing of the heart. "As the deer pants [longingly] for the water brooks, so my soul pants [longingly] for You, O God. My soul (my life, my inner self) thirsts for God, for the living God" (Psalm 42:1-2). The reality is that our soul thirsts for the living God and can only be fully satisfied and quenched by Him.

Prayer of Affirmation

As the deer pants for the water, so my soul pants longingly for You. My soul thirsts for the living God. Fill me up, Lord, full to overflow. I am willing to confront and conquer the enemy of my soul. I ask that you superimpose your will over mine. Your grace is able to make me strong in my areas of weakness. I ask You to help me to break the strongholds in my mind and will. Give me the strength when You call me to pray and fast to rid myself of 'this kind' of stronghold in my life. For I am convinced beyond any doubt that nothing shall separate me from the love of Christ, no matter what I may be experiencing in life at the moment. I am more than a conqueror and will gain an overwhelming victory in this area as I confront the enemy with your help Lord, in the name of Jesus. Thank you, Lord, for helping me as I move forward in life. Amen. (Psalm 42:1-2, 2 Corinthians 12:9-10, Matthew 17:21, Romans 8:37-39)

P

I AM PROTECTED BY THE ANGELS

For He will command His angels in regard to you, To protect and defend and guard you in all your ways [of obedience and service]. They will lift you up in their hands, So that you do not [even] strike your foot against a stone.
Psalm 91:11-12

Have you ever felt the presence of angels? Or perhaps you have had your eyes open to see into the spiritual realm to see angels. Maybe someone has shared with you a particular incident in which they were protected by an angel. I have heard stories over the years from individuals who have been divinely protected from incidents, hindrances, blocks, and accidents because of God's ministering angels. Driving up and down the dangerous highways and streets, I know that I have been protected from accidents caused by inclement weather or other drivers. Right in the moment you might say, I almost spun out of control, or that truck almost hit me. If you were to pause and reflect on why you cannot attribute "almost" to your lucky stars, you will realize you must thank God that you have angels watching over you. According to the Word of God, "He will command His angels in regard to you, To protect and defend and guard you in all your ways" (Psalm 91:11).

HIS ANGELS ARE OUR BACKUP

Angels will show up to defend you against the strategies of Satan and his demonic army. Sometimes they will move the blocks and obstacles the devil places in front of a believer. I take great comfort in knowing that they are assigned to us by God to assist us.

Are not all the angels ministering spirits sent out [by God] to serve (accompany, protect) those who will inherit salvation? [Of course they are!] (Hebrews 1:14).

If only we could see into the spiritual realm, we would understand that there are more for us than those that are against us. At times, we panic in our situation thinking we are standing alone—but we're not.

In 2 Kings, we find the account of the Syrian army attacking Israel. The army surrounded the city of Dothan, where the prophet Elisha lived. Elisha's servant became extremely terrified when he saw all of the horses and chariots surrounding them. Here's what happened:

Elisha answered, "Do not be afraid, for those who are with us are more than those who are with them." Then Elisha prayed and said, "LORD, please, open his eyes that he may see." And the LORD opened the servants eyes and he saw; and behold, the mountain was full of horses and chariots of fire surrounding Elisha.

2 Kings 6:16-17

In this passage, we learn that we are never alone in the battles against our enemies. And when we use our spiritual weapons of prayer in faith, God's angels can be released to minister healing, protection, and deliverance on our behalf. "Bless the LORD, you His angels, you mighty ones who do His commandments, obeying the voice of His word" (Psalm 103:20).

On Monday, November 30, 2015, at 6:00 a.m., I had a near miss accident on I-94 while on my way to work. Another vehicle was merging into traffic pretty fast, and it appeared as if the driver was going to hit me. All of a sudden, it was as if the car hit an invisible force or wall. When I looked into my review mirror, the car was somersaulting backwards in the air and landed right side up out of traffic and onto the shoulder of the road. I was shaken but began interceding for whoever was in the car while watching what happened. It was a miracle that the driver of the car didn't run into me and even greater that it did not land into oncoming traffic. Thank God that my angels were there to protect me. Hallelujah!

Prayer of Affirmation

Dear Father, thank you for never leaving me alone. Thank you for commanding your angels to protect, defend, and guard me. I plead the blood of Jesus to cover and protect my family, home, health, ministry, territory, land, assets, finances, business, and my life. Lord, I ask you to break all plots, schemes, and every evil tactic of the enemy sent against my life. Lord, because you are my refuge no evil or plague will come against my family, life, or house. I thank you for your angels and the strong hedge of protection that surrounds me wherever I go. In Jesus' name, amen. (Psalm 91)

I AM QUALIFIED TO SHARE IN JESUS' INHERITANCE

Giving thanks to the Father, who has qualified us to share in the inheritance of the saints (God's people) in the Light.
Colossians 1:12

TAKE UP SPIRITUAL WEAPONS FOR SPIRITUAL BATTLES

Some battles can be so fierce and heated that prayer alone is not going to provide us with the victory. When we pray, God hears and answers our prayers but sometimes the manifestation of those prayers is held up. For example, remember when Daniel had been praying and fasting for twenty-one days. His prayer was answered on the first day however; the manifestation took place twenty-one days later because of a block by a demonic principality.

Then he said to me, "Do not be afraid, Daniel, for from the first day that you set your heart on understanding this and on humbling yourself before your God, your words were heard, and I have come in response to your words. But the prince of the kingdom of Persia was standing in opposition to me for twenty-one days. Then, behold, Michael, one of the chief [of the celestial] princes, came to help me, for I had been left there with the kings of Persia.
Daniel 10:12-13

At times, we need to intensify our prayer with fasting because of the intense spiritual battles we face. However, there is warfare going on between God's angels and demons in the heavenly realms. In the Gospels, we learn that Jesus' disciples had been commissioned to cast out demons. Yet they came upon a boy with a mute spirit foaming at the mouth and were unable to cast it out.

Then one of the crowd answered and said, "Teacher, I brought You my son, who has a mute spirit. And wherever it seizes him, it throws him down; he foams at the mouth, gnashes his teeth, and becomes rigid. So I spoke to Your disciples, that they should cast it out, but they could not."

He answered him and said, "O faithless generation, how long shall I be with you? How long shall I bear with you? Bring him to Me." Then they brought him to Him. And when he saw Him, immediately the spirit convulsed him, and he fell on the ground and wallowed, foaming at the mouth. So He asked his father, "How long has this been happening to him?" And he said, "From childhood. And often he has thrown him both into the fire and into the water to destroy him. But if You can do anything, have compassion on us and help us." Jesus said to him, "If you can believe, all things are possible to him who believes." Immediately the father of the child cried out and said with tears, "Lord, I believe; help my unbelief!" When Jesus saw that the people came running together, He rebuked the unclean spirit, saying to it: "Deaf and dumb spirit, I command you, come out of him and enter him no more!" Then the spirit cried out, convulsed him greatly, and came out of him. And he became as one dead, so that many said, "He is dead." But Jesus took him by the hand and lifted him up, and he arose. And when He had come into the house, His disciples asked Him privately, "Why could we not cast it out?" So He said to them, "This kind can come out by nothing but prayer and fasting" (Mark 9:17-29).

When dealing with demons, know that there are those who are only going to be cast out through the power of prayer and fasting.

HE DID IT BEFORE–HE CAN DO IT AGAIN

When we go through periods of suffering, trials, and pain, it is not just for us to go through with the intent of wandering around or staying in our wilderness experience. Yes, I know this is easier said than done, but when suffering it helps to rest and stand on God's promise knowing that the difficult season will pass. I realize that as believers we all love the part about being heirs of God and fellow heirs with Christ as partakers of His spiritual blessings and inheritance. But along with this, we must also share in His suffering, as that is how we become stronger and powerful in Him. We endure our tests and come through with testimonies to share with others to encourage them to become overcomers. Going through a trial victoriously brings comfort and strength to others and glory to God.

And if [we are His] children, [then we are His] heirs also: heirs of God and fellow heirs with Christ [sharing His spiritual blessing and inheritance], if indeed we share in His suffering so that we may also share in His glory (Romans 8:17).

I want to share with you a trial in which I had to walk the talk by putting my spiritual weapons of prayer, fasting, and praising God into action. I understand that physicians practice medicine based upon the medical training they have received. Though many of them are not believers, the knowledge they gained still comes from God whether they believe in Him or not. Therefore, there is nothing that can supersede the miraculous healing power of the Lord, our Great Physician. The matter has been settled for the Bible says "…and with the stripes [that wounded] Him we are healed and made whole" (Isaiah 53: 5). It doesn't say we will be healed. It says we are healed because of His finished work on the cross. So that means that the outcome of what I experienced in February 2006 was set from the beginning—"And with the stripes that wounded Him I am healed and made whole"—I can honestly tell you that this Scripture was the furthest thing from my mind as I was going through pain at that time.

In February 2006, I had developed shortness of breath, a chronic cough, wheeze, and a fever. I went to the doctor to get some medicine so I could to return to work quickly. At first I began taking the medicine for influenza for about two weeks, but that didn't help. I then was placed on medicine for bronchitis. However, that didn't work either and my condition grew worse. The doctor couldn't nail down a diagnosis and had to try a variety of medicines. "I am a general practitioner, and I am testing different things to see what is going to work for you," is what he told me.

During that unimaginable situation, being confined to the upper level of my home, my husband Gary, and my boys did the best they could to take care of me. I had always been strong, healthy, independent, and vibrant. But I was reduced to someone waiting on me hand and foot because I had limited mobility. Gary and my sons were very loving and patient, bringing me anything that I needed. However, I had a difficult time accepting being flat on my back. I tried different medications and nebulizers, but instead of improving, I regressed.

After I had my fill of not getting results from this doctor, I pulled all of my medical records and started doing some research. I then went to a pulmonologist (a doctor specializing in respiratory diseases) seeking a solution. She was going to prescribe the steroid prednisone for an incurable disease called sarcoidosis. But I refused to accept her diagnosis and told her, "I don't have that." I knew not to claim that illness as mine. Besides, that was just the latest diagnosis I received among the others such as lymphadenopathy and interstitial disease. Because I wouldn't accept that report, I only discussed with my immediate family, my pastor, and the pastor's wife.

So why did I take the medication? I was looking for a quick fix to be able to return to work. When I asked her about the side effects what jumped out at me was weight gain and osteoarthritis. I couldn't imagine putting weight on my 5 foot 2 inch frame. So I compromised and told her that I would take the medicine every other day.

Spiritually speaking, do you realize the devil comes in many forms? It's not always about tempting you to commit adultery or sins of that nature. The devil tries to get you to doubt God. Let me be clear, I am not saying that the doctor is the devil. However, I am saying that the devil comes to kill, steal, and destroy, and he was looking to take me out—if not through the sickness, then through the medicine with all of its terrible side effects. God allowed me to see I was under a spiritual attack. We are not ignorant to the devil's devices. The enemy uses incurable diseases as a tactic to bring destruction.

I could identify with the woman who had an issue of blood twelve years. "And who had endured much suffering under [the hands of] many physicians and had spent all that she had, and was no better but instead grew worse" (Mark 5:26). I thank God that it was only after giving a testimony at church on the power of prayer and fasting, that I eventually came to myself.

Earlier, I mentioned my oldest son, Aaron, was diagnosed with the symptoms of asthma and the doctor wanted him to be on the steroid Albuterol. The doctors were telling me that he had asthma and would probably have to receive breathing treatments indefinitely. After having listened to healing Scriptures on tape over and over again, there was no doubt and I believed my son was healed of asthma—so much so, that I decided to go on a three-day Esther fast (no food or water for three days and three nights).

I had faith that God had healed my son, so I put away the breathing machine when I got home after a Friday night Watch Service. I released my faith by an action. For according to James,

So also faith, if it does not have works (deeds and actions of obedience to back it up), by itself is destitute of power (inoperative, dead). It's still faith but it's dead. James went on to say, But someone will say [to you then], You [say you] have faith, and

I have [good] works. Now you show me your [alleged] faith apart from any [good] works [if you can], and I by [good] works [of obedience] will show you my faith.

James 2:18

I took action. The spiritual medicine that Aaron began to take every day was this: "Thank you, Jesus, that by your stripes I am healed." God gets all of the glory for healing my son, and I have had many opportunities to share with others the power of God to deliver through prayer and fasting.

On one occasion, when my youngest son Laurence was a newborn, I took him to the doctor for a routine check-ups. It was during this visit that the doctor diagnosed him with a heart murmur. Well my mind immediately went back to what God had done with Aaron. I asked God what should I do? He led me to do a five-day liquid fast to believe Him for total healing. During the fast, I anointed and prayed over Laurence. During the next appointment, the doctor examined Laurence and could find no evidence of a heart murmur. My sons are fifteen and twenty now, and both have been healthy to this day with the exception of a seasonal cold or flu-like symptoms.

So now fast forward to me having shared these powerful healing testimonials with the congregation at my church, I began to walk to my seat and the Holy Spirit said to me as I returned to my seat, "Since you believed that I could heal your sons, can you believe that I can heal you?" WOW, this indeed hit me like a bolt of lightning. Wait a minute; I know I'm not in the boat all by myself. Why is it that we can always believe God so strongly for other people? Yet when it comes to praying and trusting that God can come through for us we waver. I had to stop and realize from the testimonials of healing for my sons that if God did it before then He is well able to do it again. He miraculously healed both of my sons of generational curses that were passed down from each side of my family, with asthma on my dad's side of the family and heart murmurs on my mom's side of the family. Those curses were cut off once and for all! So as I sat down in my seat and really listened to the words that I said about the power of God to heal, I realized I had to believe that God would do it for me.

In addition, I heeded the voice of the Lord to tell no one about me stopping to take any of my prescribed medications. With having taken only three tablets, I put the bottle away. I felt in my heart that if I continued taking the medicine and was overtaken by side effects, it would start a vicious cycle of taking medication to continually cure the side effects. Later the same day, I was reading a devotional that included this passage of Scripture:

When He had reached the house and went in, the blind men came to Him, and Jesus said to them, Do you believe that I am able to do this? They said to Him, Yes, Lord. Then He touched their eyes, saying, According to your faith and trust and reliance [on the power invested in Me] be it done to you; And their eyes were opened. Jesus earnestly and sternly charged them, See that you let no one know about this.
Matthew 9:28-30

This was a faith walk that I was supposed to do alone. That meant I wasn't to share anything about what I was going to do with my husband, my parents, or my pastor. Like the woman who had an issue of blood, I too had to press into Jesus.

For she kept saying, If I only touch His garments, I shall be restored to health. And immediately her flow of blood was dried up at the source, and [suddenly] she felt in her body that she was healed of her [distressing] ailment.
Mark 5:28-29

In March 2006, I began a 21-day liquid fast because I wanted to rid my body of all toxins from the medication that I had in my system and believe God for divine healing. I followed a daily regimen of speaking "healing Scriptures" throughout the day along with singing praise and worship songs. My favorite passage to meditate on was Jeremiah 17:14, which reads, "heal me, O Lord, and I shall be healed; save me, and I shall be saved; for thou art my praise." Faith without works is dead and to put what God was doing in my life to the test, my mom called and after we prayed together she gave me a word of encouragement and shared that I should go to the basement to praise the Lord. I took heed to the instructions and went down two flights of stairs and gave God a radical praise as a shout unto the Lord with a voice of triumph. When I returned to the upper level, I was no longer short of breath. Hallelujah! I began to feel stronger and could go up and down the stairs in my household without becoming winded. Not long after that, my mom and I began doing 4-mile walks. I then returned to work on a part-time basis in April 2006. Thank God that I too was made whole, as the Great Physician healed my body.

Many are the afflictions of the righteous: but the LORD delivereth him out of them all (Psalm 34:19).

So what happened when I returned back to the pulmonologist in June 2006? The pulmonologist took a look at my chest x-rays and my breathing level had dramatically changed for the better, and she couldn't believe the improvement. My blood pressure reading was 114/72, pulse and respiration was 100/56, and I was 16 pounds lighter. She stated, "Lauretha what did you do, it looks like we can taper the dose for the prednisone?" I mentioned to her that I fasted, prayed, did holistic treatments of natural herbs, rested, and exercised. Her ears perked up to question "What type of herbs did you take?" I shared with her the natural herbs that I took and of course she didn't ask anything further about my spiritual remedy. She gave me a prescription to continue the Prednisone medication that I immediately discarded when I went out the door, never to return.

In October 2008, I continued to see the pulmonologist in my travels because we treat patients together on a professional basis. I knew that the Lord healed me on day one, and I just waited on the manifestation. I thank and praise and give glory to God for being my Great Physician.

So, why did I go through this particular test? To declare through Christ Jesus that I am victorious and that God causes me to always triumph. **And they have overcome (conquered) him (devil) by means of the blood of the Lamb and by the utterance of their testimony (Revelation 12:11).**

I have been able to share this testimony at my church as I placed the prescription bottle on the altar. Giving God the glory in my healing ministered to others in the congregation who were diagnosed with incurable diseases and currently taking prednisone or knew someone who was. God is not a respecter of persons, and since He was able to heal me He can heal others of any sickness, malady, or disease. The Bible says, "the Lord heals [each one of] all your diseases" (Psalm 103:3). This has also been a way to share my faith, recite my testimony, pray, and lay hands on the sick. My testimony has been a tool to witness to others in the marketplace to lead them to our Great Physician. For when you endure and overcome, you gain experience and then are able to teach others. People can always learn from and be encouraged by someone who has been where they are stationed or going. I encourage others to share and give testimony to what God is doing or has done in their life. You never know the impact you may have on someone's life for healing, deliverance, and breakthrough. I praise God for almost ten years that I've been medication-free. I'm a strong believer in natural holistic remedies. Since God created us as living beings from the dust (minerals) of the earth, it makes sense that it would take whole foods and minerals, along with fitness, to maintain our health.

Healing the sick is God's will. Jesus says, "For I have come down from heaven not to do My own will and purpose but to do the will and purpose of Him Who sent Me" (John 6:38).

He personally bore our sins in His [own] body on the tree [as on an altar and offered Himself on it], that we might die (cease to exist) to sin and live to righteousness. By His wounds you have been healed.

1 Peter 2:24

The afflictions in our body were laid upon Jesus, and He bore them. Recognize that we do not need to carry or bear them. This is a statement of fact that by Jesus' stripes, we have been healed. This is not something that is going to happen to us but has already happened. We just need to accept what we have already received in faith—by Jesus' stripes, we are already healed.

I have become a firm believer in prayer prevention or preemptive praying along with fasting. Shortly after attending a seminar at my church for a season every day before leaving my home, I laid hands on Gary, Aaron, Laurence, and myself to command that our immune systems be fully restored to normal function. I learned this from Charles and Frances Hunter's Handbook for Healing. It is a powerful and effective tool that I utilize daily in my household and in the marketplace. As a person that lives by faith, it is wonderful to watch God confirm His Word by performing healing and sometimes miracles before my very eyes. My response is always one of gratitude and giving glory to God. For all the glory and honor belongs to Him alone, who is so worthy, awesome, and faithful to His Word. Imagine as every believer puts into practice this word for your household, ministry, marketplace, etc… Jesus stated, "And these signs shall follow them that believe;… they shall lay hands on the sick, and they shall recover" (Mark 16:17-18).

Prayer of Affirmation

God, I thank you for the power of prayer and fasting to break the power of every kind of sickness and disease in my life. I bind the works of the enemy and any attack over my life. I command every spirit of affliction, disease, and disorder to come out of my body. I command every electrical, magnetic, and chemical frequency to align itself in my body to work in proper order. I command all of the good cells in my body to overpower and digest all of the bad cells in my body, in Jesus name. I thank you and praise you for my healing, Lord. I thank you that by Jesus' stripes I am already healed. I thank you that as a believer I shall lay hands on the sick, and they shall recover. I expect the supernatural. In Jesus' name, amen. (Jeremiah 17:14, I Peter 2:24, St. Mark 16:17-18)

Rest

Part 5

YOU ARE CHOSEN BY HIS DESIGN

I AM THE RIGHTEOUSNESS OF GOD

He made Christ who knew no sin to [judicially] be sin on our behalf, so that in Him we would become the righteousness of God [that is, we would be made acceptable to Him and placed in a right relationship with Him by His gracious lovingkindness].
2 Corinthians 5:21

GOD DESIRES INTIMACY

Have you ever been in an unhealthy relationship with a friend? Do you have a hard time developing healthy boundaries in relationships? Have you ever thought of pursuing a current relationship so that it goes from good to great? Many of you answered "yes" to all of the above. We all thrive in wanting to make our relationships with others the best they can be. But the ultimate relationship is our connection with our Father. That is really what we were created for. We are meant to be in right standing and right relationship with Him. The key is making it just as personal as we do with our family and friends. I don't know about you, but for many years I struggled with trying to do the right thing to have a relationship with God. When in actuality I just needed to believe right. What I mean by that is, it took me many years before I really understood His new covenant message of grace. I realized that God is not waiting to condemn me every time I miss the mark. My sins are forgiven and remembered no more because of Jesus' ultimate sacrifice.

Because of Jesus' sacrifice, God's holiness and righteousness has already been satisfied and fully paid for concerning my sins past, present, and future. I am so glad that God is not keeping a record of all my sins and that it gives me the freedom to boldly come before Him to the throne of grace with no guilt or condemnation. "For I will be merciful and gracious toward their wickedness, And I will remember their sins no more" (Hebrews 8:12). Through my personal relationship with Jesus Christ, I discovered that God is a loving and forgiving Father. He wants me to be in communication with Him where we spend quality time together. It is the same as you do with the people you love. You desire to communicate and get to know them better. God desires intimacy from each of us because He has so much to share with us to direct and guide our path.

Also in this process I get to know Him better and what pleases His heart. And our relationship grows stronger and better as I find myself talking to Him throughout the day. In Jeremiah 33:3, His Word encourages us to "Call to Me and I will answer you, and tell you [and even show you] great and mighty things, [things which have been confined and hidden], which you do not know and understand and cannot distinguish." I need God to help me take the guesswork out of what I should do, say, or where to go. I do believe that His direction and favor saves us from much unnecessary labor and hardship.

I start my day with prayer in thanksgiving, praise, and intercession. Through the course of my day, I am asking for His wisdom, guidance, and knowledge as to what to do and say when I work with my clients, or out and about in the marketplace, and with my family. I ask for confidence, strength, and boldness to stand in challenging situations. I close my day with thanksgiving to my loving Father not as a perfunctory ritual but as an ongoing, interactive, right relationship with Him. He has been so good that I can't help but to bless Him and thank Him for who He is, what He has done, and praise Him in advance for what He is going to do.

Prayer of Affirmation

Because of Jesus finished work on the cross in taking the penalty for all of my sins past, present, and future I am forgiven. I come to you, Father, boldly before the throne of grace with expectation that you hear and answer my prayers. I ask for the spirit of wisdom, revelation knowledge, and understanding to know you better. Give me greater insight and vision for my life, my family, ministry, business, and career. Give me clarity of knowing how to move in your timing and with strategy to impact all whom you place in my life today by divine appointment. I want to love as you love. Fill my heart full to overflow with more of you. I decrease that You may increase in me more of your goodness, loving kindness, peace, joy, strength, self-control, and faithfulness. I desire to draw closer and know you better. More than anything, I want to be made more in your image. Less of me and more of you is my heart's cry. In Jesus' name, amen. (Ephesians 1:17, John 3:30, Galatians 5:22-23, Ephesians 4:24)

I AM STRONG IN THE LORD

Have I not commanded you? Be strong and courageous! Do not be terrified or dismayed (intimidated), for the LORD your God is with you wherever you go.
Joshua 1:9

SILENT NO MORE

In the heat of the battle when the attack is prolonged we find ourselves wondering if it will ever end. We even begin to question God. How long must I suffer in pain? Why me? Going through our tests, we really cannot understand the full picture. I believe that it takes coming out on the other side to come to the full knowledge of why you went through. More often than not, you will discover it is not about us per se but about the testing of our faith. This revelation may come right away or it could be years before you fully realize that ultimately what you have gone through is to be a testimony that will bring God glory.

For I consider [from the standpoint of faith] that the sufferings of the present life are not worthy to be compared with the glory that is about to be revealed to us and in us!
Romans 8:18

At this point in my life, I thought I'd never be sharing my story of being abused. For many years now, being abused caused me so many problems in my life. I went to therapy and released it to God. For many years I struggled with the pain (and later the bitterness and anger) of suffering in silence. I had battled with thoughts of suicide in my teenage years. I felt that I could never be good enough and was ashamed of what had happened to me. Someone I trusted as an adult took advantage of me in my youth. I felt led to get counseling before getting married so that it would not have any adverse effects on my relationship with my husband. I was apprehensive about having children. I told the therapist and Gary that I did not want what happened to me as a youth to be passed on in my bloodline.

Before getting married, I was able to forgive the individual who sexually abused me. In his own sick insanity, he thought that sex with a relative was normal because he had also been raised in a dysfunctional, incestuous environment. Finally, the curse of incest in my generation and moving forward was broken in my family. Unfortunately, my immediate family was scattered and have not been close for many years. On Sunday, November 29, 2015, while at dinner with my mother, I shared my desire to see our family be close once again, but I just didn't know how that was going to happen. This had been my mom's prayer for many years. Then the next day on November 30, 2015, when I was praying early that morning, the Lord spoke to my heart. He said, "Ask your mother and brother to attend a one-night revival." The revival was being held at my church, with the speaker being my First Lady Bonita A. Shelby. They did come and what happened that night was beyond amazing.

Afterwards when I spoke with my mom and brother, we all testified that both Pastor Don W. Shelby Jr. and his wife shared our story from beginning to end. The service ended with prophetic words being released and a powerful prayer of deliverance for the breaking of curses off our families, bodies, and finances. We all walked out of that service with the curse of separation being broken off our family and the beginning of restoration taking place. I shared with Dad and Mom Shelby that my mom, siblings, and I had a family meeting and God had supernaturally restored what the enemy had stolen all of those years ago. We were able to pick up and laugh, and talk, and plan how we were going to move forward as a family. The process is not complete, but in due season we will have a testimony.

And I will compensate you for the years that the swarming locust has eaten, the creeping locust, the stripping locust, and the gnawing locust—My great army which I sent among you (Joel 2:25).

I am so thankful and grateful to God to know that it is never too late for things to turnaround, to work out for the better and in our favor. Looking back I can see the way it happened was in God's perfect timing.

CHRIST HIMSELF WILL STRENGTHEN YOU

You're saying what about my past? I too, went through the pain of being abused, talked about, lied on, money taken and never returned, mistreated, judged, and ridiculed by those who were closest to me. I thought that because they were my family, friends, or acquaintances that couldn't possibly be happening to me. I said it earlier in the book, and I'm going to say it again. You were designed with purpose to please God and bring Him glory in the earth. Do not allow yourself to stop short of focusing on that goal. What took place in your past doesn't define your future! Let it go and keep pressing into the call and purpose of your future. God is behind the scenes fighting your unseen enemies. You cannot be silent in your pain and suffering anymore. Reach out to someone who can offer you spiritual counseling and social support so that generational curse that you are fighting can be broken. We were not created to be victims of our circumstances; instead, we are victorious in Him and through Him.

After you have suffered for a little while, the God of all grace [who imparts His blessing and favor], who called you to His own eternal glory in Christ, will Himself complete, confirm, strengthen, and establish you [making you what you ought to be.
1 Peter 5:10

It is my prayer that God will give you the supernatural grace to be delivered, healed, and strengthened. You are more powerful than you know.

I can do all things [which He has called me to do] through Him who strengthens and empowers me [to fulfill His purpose—I am self-sufficient in Christ's sufficiency; I am ready for anything and equal to anything through Him who infuses me with inner strength and confident peace.]
Philippians 4:13

Prayer of Affirmation

God, I was designed and created with purpose to please you and bring you glory in the earth. I declare that I can do all things you have called me to do through Jesus Christ, who strengthens and empowers me to fulfill Your purpose. I am ready to go forth in my calling and purpose as you infuse me with inner strength and confident peace. I have great expectation of good things coming my way even if I have been a victim of my life circumstances. My past does not define me. And after I have suffered a little while, your supernatural grace will flood to impart your blessings and favor. Father, I believe you will complete, confirm, strengthen, and establish me to make me what I ought to be. You will compensate me for the years the locust has eaten from me. You will restore sevenfold for every second, hour, and year that has been stripped from me suddenly as if it were never lost. I will recover all of my joy, peace, happiness, anointing, and divine health, in the mighty name of Jesus. Though I sow in tears, I shall reap in joy. In Jesus' name, Amen. (Philippians 4:13, I Peter 5:10, Joel 2:25, Psalm 126:5)

I AM THE TEMPLE OF THE HOLY SPIRIT

Do you not know that your body is a temple of the Holy Spirit who is within you, whom you have [received as a gift] from God, and that you are not your own [property]?
1 Corinthians 6:19

I am letting this sink in right now: my body is the temple of the Holy Spirit. When I think of this, my mind goes back to a familiar Bible passage that speaks of various leaders who built or worshiped at the temple. It was a physical place to go and spend time in the presence of God to worship and adore Him for who He is and praise Him for what He has already done and will do in our lives. King Solomon constructed an elaborate temple to worship God, and his temple was unique in that there were no idols. Phoenician craftsmen had a huge task in building the temple, which began in the fourth year of Solomon's reign and took seven years to complete. Although Solomon built the temple Scripture reveals that God did not need to make this His physical dwelling place. But it was Solomon who built a house for Him. However, the Most High [the One infinitely exalted above humanity] does not dwell in houses made by human hands; as the prophet [Isaiah] says, "HEAVEN IS MY THRONE, AND THE EARTH IS THE FOOTSTOOL FOR MY FEET; WHAT KIND OF HOUSE WILL YOU BUILD FOR ME?' says the Lord, 'OR WHAT PLACE IS THERE FOR MY REST? WAS IT NOT MY HAND THAT MADE ALL THESE THINGS?'"(Acts 7:47-50)

He owns everything and has made everything here on earth and does not need to live in a place made by human hands. "The God who created the world and everything in it, since He is Lord of heaven and earth, does not dwell in temples made with hands" (Acts 17:24).

WE NEED HELP EVERY HOUR OF EVERY DAY

Yet we need God to be connected to us and to live on the inside of us. A lot of times we don't even recognize the significance of why we fully need Him. He chose us and desires to be so connected to us that He sent the Helper, which is the Holy Spirit, to live inside us.

But the Helper (Comforter, Advocate, Intercessor—Counselor, Strengthener, Standby), the Holy Spirit, whom the Father will send in My name [in My place, to represent Me and act on My behalf], He will teach you all things. And He will help you remember everything that I have told you.

John 14:26

It is in my nature to be independent. However, when I need an answer to a problem I am dealing with, I depend on help from the Holy Spirit. I realize it is not only being dependent on the Holy Spirit for the big problems, but it is also depending upon Him for the most minute situations of our lives as well that is critical. We are not our own to just do anything we please. We cannot just say anything we want or go any place we want to go. Why not? We belong to Him. We are God's property.

Do you not know that your body is a temple of the Holy Spirit who is within you, whom you have [received as a gift] from God, and that you are not your own [property]? (1 Corinthians 6:19).

The Holy Spirit, who lives in each believer is a gift from God. Therefore, we have to be careful about what we do with our temple. Just think about if you were to have the President of the United States come to your house for dinner. Wouldn't you have your house thoroughly cleaned and straightened up? You would certainly set out your best dishes, have flowers on display, and serve your absolute best meal. Though the President deserves due honor and respect, He is not God. He did not give us breath or life. Yes, we can honor the president but it is God alone who deserves our worship. God is our heavenly Father, who loves us so much that He gave His very best to us. He gave His one and only Son, Jesus, to be Savior and Lord over our lives. Secondly, He did not leave us without help as we go along on our journey.

Through the Spirit, God gives each believer a measure of faith and spiritual gifts for service to the Lord. It is His desire that we activate and utilize the gifts the Holy Spirit graces us to have. The purpose of these gifts are to comfort, encourage, and build up the body of Christ. We are also to witness to win others to Christ and build up each other in the body of Christ. What an awesome, loving Father who looks to include us in His kingdom work! As we spend time meditating and learning Scriptures the Holy Spirit is there to lead and guide us into all truth, and bring back to our remembrance what we have learned from Scripture. This is why it is so important to have Scripture planted deep inside your heart. How else can the Holy Spirit bring back to remembrance something that was never there? Yes, I've learned and committed Scriptures to memory over the years, but I need to continually do this. I'll admit I have not been as diligent in this area as I need to be. I am re-committing to Bible study and Scripture memory because I know that this is where my help and strength come from. However, I will not fall into condemnation if I miss studying according to my scheduled plan. I recognize that, by grace, this life is a journey of continued growth.

But grow [spiritually mature] in the grace and knowledge of our Lord and Savior Jesus Christ.

2 Peter 3:18

We will never obtain complete perfection in this life, but we continue to strive becoming more like Him day by day. Thank God that we can draw from the comfort, guidance, and strength of the Helper—Holy Spirit.

Prayer of Affirmation

Father, thank you for the gift of the Holy Spirit living in me. I rely and depend on the Holy Spirit every moment of each day to be my helper, comforter, advocate, intercessor, counselor, strengthener, and to be right there by my side in the time of need. He will teach me all things and help me to remember everything I have learned from you. Help me to fully use the gifts within the Holy Spirit that you have given me to bless, comfort, encourage, build up, witness to, and serve others. It is my desire with the help of Holy Spirit to continue to grow spiritually strong in the grace and knowledge of my Lord and Savior Jesus Christ. In Jesus' name, amen. (Corinthians 6:19, John 14:26, I Corinthians 14, 2 Peter 3:18)

U

I AM UNIQUE AND CHOSEN BY GOD

For you are a holy people [set apart] to the LORD your God; and the LORD has chosen you out of all the peoples who are on the earth to be a people for His own possession
Deuteronomy 14:2

God chose you. Isn't that something amazing to ponder? If you are anything like me, you may wonder how and why He would have chosen you. Maybe you think, What do I have to offer God with all my flaws and frailties? Do you sometimes feel like a broken and empty vessel? Are you the type of person who pours so much of yourself into others that you barely have any anything left for yourself? If you answered yes to any or all of the above, do not despair, help is on the way.

No matter what we have been through, or what stage of life we are in, we are still chosen by God, even if it doesn't feel like it. We are vessels fit for the Master to use—all for His glory. A vessel that is fit is a suitable quality or type to meet the required purpose. Though we are all different, yet each of us has something in common, we have a God-given purpose, a unique quality and gifting that God desires to use for us to impact and influence others for the greater good. We all have had different experiences in life that have molded and shaped our personalities, belief systems, morals, and attitudes. Since God's Word declares it, than that settles the matter that you are uniquely chosen by God.

For you are a holy people [set apart] to the LORD your God; and the LORD has chosen you out of all the peoples who are on the earth to be a people for His own possession.

Deuteronomy 14:2

It is of great comfort to know that nothing can happen in our lives that's not part of God's plan for our lives. Whether good, bad, or ugly, there are no accidents. God cannot be surprised by things that happen to you. The Bible says, " For I know the plans and thoughts that I have for you,' says the LORD, 'plans for peace and well-being and not for disaster to give you a future and a hope" (Jeremiah 29:11). God is the potter and we are the clay. When God formed us, He gave us our talents, gifts, and uniqueness. When I look back over my life I can see the many challenges and pitfalls I endured. Those events became the basis for my testimony, which I could share with someone else to bring comfort, strength, and encouragement. When I share stories of His strength and power through areas in which I've been blessed to have healing and deliverance, I realize that it is important that God gets all the glory. Some testimonies were easier to share, but each time I see someone who is suffering if there is any way in which I can share to offer an encouraging word or prayer, I will speak up.

It is good to know that unlike people, God does not discard us over our issues. Being broken, depleted, and empty vessels doesn't disqualify us from receiving Christ's abundance. I think those who have experienced the greatest trials are ripe for being used by God. Our deliverance exemplifies His faithfulness, love, and redeeming grace. We have so many examples in biblical history: Noah was a drunk, Abraham was old and impotent, Jacob was a liar, Moses had a stuttering problem, Gideon was afraid, Rahab was a prostitute, David was an adulterer and murderer, the Samaritan woman was divorced five times, and Martha worried about everything. All those biblical characters were flawed individuals just like you and I. Yet, God chose them to impact a flawed world.

Just look at your own calling, believers; not many [of you were considered] wise according to human standards, not many powerful or influential, not many of high and noble birth. But God has selected [for His purpose] the foolish things of the world to shame the wise [revealing their ignorance], and God has selected [for His purpose] the weak things of the world to shame the things which are strong [revealing their frailty].

1 Corinthians 1:26-27

Isn't it great to know that despite not being the greatest according to human standards, that God has called and chosen us to do His work?

I AM CHOSEN FOR GREATNESS

Repeatedly, I say to myself: "don't care what people think. I think only about pleasing Him. I am uniquely chosen of God." It's amazing how when you rehearse something (your true identity) you begin to attract that thing to you. In addition, those around you will mirror what you say or do. On more than one occasion, I have heard my sons talk about greatness in term of their destiny. I constantly speak these subjects over their lives. Now it has become a part of their reality. Therefore, let me speak over your life too.

You too are chosen for an extraordinary life and greatness. There is nothing mediocre or ordinary about you because we serve an extraordinary supernatural God. Believe that wherever you walk in life, He is able to place His super on top of your natural. What you've been chosen to do for Him, He has already equipped you to do. I have always had a passion for reading books, teaching, writing, and trying new recipes, that's why doing or enjoying those activities are easy for me to do. Whatever your passion, therein can your calling, purpose and destiny be found.

Writing my testimonies has always been a part of His purpose for me. This was confirmed when my spiritual dad and pastor gave me a prophetic word. Initially, when he said the word "memoirs" three times, I thought he meant I would be telling his story, not mine. It took a year-and-a-half to execute the plan to start writing. All I know is that I have had some difficult events occur in my life coupled with a faulty belief system. But thank God for realizing my true identity as one who has been accepted as His beloved daughter.

During the fall of 2015, I opened a new chapter in my life concerning my journey in the Lord. I am glad that I made the sacrifice to draw closer to Him in my quiet time. I so enjoy being in His presence. Sometimes I have to fight hugging my pillow a little longer over getting up to pray right away. However, once I am up and in His presence, He brings such joy and peace to quench my thirsty soul. As I continue my spiritual journey with spiritual counseling along with much prayer and fasting, I can live out my best life, which is to help my family and others. As we increase in knowledge and grace, we are transformed into who God intended us to be.

You have not chosen Me, but I have chosen you and I have appointed and placed and purposefully planted you, so that you would go and bear fruit and keep on bearing, and that your fruit will remain and be lasting, so that whatever you ask of the Father in My name [as My representative] He may give to you.

John 15:16

Prayer of Affirmation

I am holy and set apart to you, Lord. I have flaws and imperfections, but you can use me because You are perfect in all of your ways. And I am complete in you. Thank you for uniquely choosing me. I know the plans and thoughts that you think toward me. They are plans for peace and well-being and not for disaster to give me a future and a hope. Please give me the courage to walk away from the roles and expectations that other people have for me. I desire to live in peace and contentment exactly the way you created me to be. I desire to live my life on purpose and for your designed purpose. By design appointment and divine assignment I will be able to encourage, strengthen, and give comfort to those whom He associated me with in my spheres of influence. I have a unique talent, gift, abilities, or testimony that I am anointed to minister to serve in love to your people to bring you glory. I decrease that you may increase more of your grace, strength, and loving kindness in me and through me. In Jesus' name, thank you. Amen. (Deuteronomy 14:2, Colossians 2:10, Jeremiah 29:11, John 3:30)

V

I AM VICTORIOUS THROUGH CHRIST

*Do not fear [anything], for I am with you; Do not be afraid, for I am your God.
I will strengthen you, be assured I will help you; I will certainly take hold of you with
My righteous right hand [a hand of justice, of power, of victory, of salvation].*
Isaiah 41:10

Have you ever tried to do things in your own strength only to find out that your strength wasn't nearly enough? Even though you were qualified to accomplish the task, you still came up short. Well, that's because God doesn't want us to attempt to complete a task in our own strength, where we end up getting frustrated and settling for less than doing our best. Doing so only leads to us dropping it prematurely. However, God wants us to be led by His Spirit to have success that has been divinely orchestrated for us to achieve. All of our success in life comes from us being in kingdom alignment in order for the blessings of God's perfect will to be manifested in our lives.

STRATEGY FOR SUCCESS

What is a good strategy for success? What comes to mind is when Moses died and Joshua became the leader of Israel—3 million people strong. Even by today's standards, that was a formidable task. Imagine orchestrating the day-to-day operations of so many people, many of whom were fearful doubters and complainers. God knew that Joshua was going to need His assistance. So He gave Joshua the blueprint for winning all of his future battles with success. He told him to meditate day and night on His Word and to do what it says.

This Book of the Law shall not depart from your mouth, but you shall read [and meditate on] it day and night, so that you may be careful to do [everything] in accordance with all that is written in it; for then you will make your way prosperous, and then you will be successful.

Joshua 1:8

Joshua takes heed to God's instruction and finds himself winning every battle. His focus was on magnifying God's Word and not the situation. I can imagine him saying, "I am victorious. I am strong in the Lord. I am more than a conqueror. I am protected by angels. I am empowered to successfully engage in spiritual warfare and achieve victory." What challenges are you facing today? Are you facing giants of an eviction notice, foreclosure, unemployment, tremendous debt, a challenging boss, a divorce, or a disease in your body? God has given us a key to help win every battle. We are to meditate on His Word day and night. We are to speak and shout the victory NOW over our situation to see good success. God reassures us to have no fear of that thing because He is right there with us in the midst of what we are going through.

Do not fear [anything], for I am with you; do not be afraid, for I am your God. I will strengthen you, be assured I will help you; I will certainly take hold of you with My righteous right hand [a hand of justice, of power, of victory, of salvation].

Isaiah 41:10

DON'T LOSE THE BATTLE OF THE MIND

Yep the real warfare begins in the mind. It is a battle from the attack of thoughts and imaginations that seek to set up strongholds in your thinking. Usually what we spend a lot of time thinking about never even comes to pass. That person is talking about me, my boss is planning to fire me, or I just know he is going to leave me. So often we waste our time when we allow our imaginations to run wild. Constant mind chatter causes people to stop dead in their tracks instead of becoming all that God has purposed them to be. It is important that we realize that we are all engaged in spiritual warfare on the battlefield of the mind. Every day we need to focus our minds on good things to come, such as the promises of God. If not, our minds will focus on a memory of the past to try to get us to change course and go back to what we were delivered from. Remember what happened to Israel in the wilderness? Many of them wanted to return to Egypt. It is for this reason that the past should remain dead and buried.

It is so important to have positive pictures to focus on. Get a dream board or create a vision board where you write down your visions and dreams so you can meditate over them again and again. Do you have as a role model, mentor, leader, or teacher who is in the place where you desire to go in your career, ministry, or business? My pastor and his wife are my spiritual mentors. They lead by example by demonstrating love for family; being prayer warriors; having integrity; and being good teachers, excellent counselors, and fervent praisers. I shared in detail earlier the tremendous help I've had with dynamic mentors and coaches in my online business.

In addition to all the aforementioned, we need to constantly feed our minds with godly things because it will cause us to prosper and be better at whatever God called us to do. Reading ten pages or listening to an audio book for ten minutes every day to feed the mind something positive, encouraging, and inspirational can be life changing. We need a "mind shape up" talk every day—meaning we need to talk to God and shape our minds around what His Words says about us. And that's why I began each day with my ABCs of positive affirmations as I stand in my bathroom mirror. My mind shapes up to who God says I am, what He says I can do, and who He says I can become. I keep reminders in several places—post-it notes are on my computer, in my car, on the wall in my workspace to remind me to confess throughout my day, what thus saith Lord. Over the years, I have been attacked by negative thoughts and imaginations, but I have determined not to lose the battle of my mind. I've learned that I need to hear from the Lord not for big problems but for the little ones as well. I am never far from success when I allow the leading of the Holy Spirit to direct my course in life. **But thanks be to God, who always leads us in triumph in Christ (2 Corinthians 2:14).**

Prayer of Affirmation

Father, I'm so sorry that I've lived a lot of my life guided by my own direction and getting ahead of your timing. You have been there to offer me guidance, power, and wisdom. I desire to look to you for instruction and leading me to victory. I will have no fear of anything for you are with me. You will strengthen me and help me in every battle. You will certainly take hold of me with your righteous right hand of justice, of power, of victory, and of salvation. I am coming out on top. I am strong in you. I am more than a conqueror. Thank you,, God, for always causing me to triumph in Christ. Thank you, in Jesus' name. Amen. (Isaiah 41:10, Ephesians 6:10, Romans 8:31-39, 2 Corinthians 2:14)

I AM FEARFULLY AND WONDERFULLY MADE

I will give thanks and praise to You, for I am fearfully and wonderfully made; Wonderful are Your works, And my soul knows it very well.
Psalm 139:14

At some point in your life, have you thought about changing some attribute of your body? Do you wish you were shorter or taller? Perhaps you wanted to be a few shades lighter or darker. I told you about my wish at the beginning of this book. The list is endless of all the things we would like to do to change our bodily appearance. Cosmetics is a multi-billion dollar industry simply because people want to alter the way they look (not to mention breast implants and the latest craze of butt injections). But wait a minute, are we really saying we don't appreciate the way we were fashioned by our Creator. Didn't He make us? Doesn't His word say that we are fearfully and wonderfully made? Then why do we try to transform into something He didn't make. It goes back again to identifying with what the world has us to model.

When growing up, so many girls tried to identify with the dolls they played with such as Barbie. The problem was, Barbie only represented one aspect of beauty based upon Caucasian standards of beauty. There was no diversity. Girls of color felt they could not measure up to the white standards of beauty being of a brown or black complexion. So how did that cause young girls to respond? Unfortunately, it caused low self-esteem in girls of color, because being black or brown, they could never measure up to being beautiful by white standards.

I have nothing against Barbie, especially since they have added diversity to the Barbie Doll product line. They have added girls who are petite, curvy, and tall with different skin tones, eye colors, and facial features. Why? so informed people of color would continue to buy their products. Intelligent consumers want products that embrace their cultural uniqueness. Finally, the toy manufacturers caught on.

Much of the stress people go through would be eliminated if they didn't try to adjust to constantly changing social trends. We are not to be imitators of the world but imitators of the Word. We are to take on the identity of Christ. This is where many Christians struggle. We all want to be accepted, which means we try to conform to the ways of the world. We have to see ourselves as beautiful and wonderfully made just as we are. God did not make a mistake when he gave us curly hair, big lips, or a small stature. He designed each of us perfectly and uniquely. He individually broke the mold when He made you and me in His image. It was all a part of His plan and purpose for our lives. So who are we to try to fix what He fashioned? You have to have boldness and confidence and not be afraid of accepting yourself. You are fearfully and wonderfully made in God's image.

I will give thanks and praise to You, for I am fearfully and wonderfully made; wonderful are Your works, and my soul knows it very well.
Psalm 139:14

Just as a vinedresser prunes and purges his grapevines so they will produce good fruit, so does our heavenly Father prunes, purges, and positions us in a process to bear great fruit for His kingdom. Though pruning and purging are not comfortable, we cannot give up in the middle of the process. We have to be teachable and willing to listen to instructions and receive the correction that He gives us. Therefore, we should focus on His plan and purpose for us and not so quickly try to conform to the false images the world portrays.

One of my favorite "she-roes" in the Bible is Queen Esther, a woman whom I admire for her courage, strength, elegance, and beauty. Esther was an intercessor, courageous and strategically positioned to work God's plan to deliver the Jews. She was a woman of prayer and fasting. When the Jews were facing genocide, it was time for Esther to stand up. Though in Medo-Persian law it was a death sentence for anyone to approach the king unsummoned, her uncle Mordecai reminded her that perhaps she was just where God wanted her to be "for such a time as this."

Then Mordecai told them to reply to Esther, "Do not imagine that you in the king's palace can escape any more than all the Jews. For if you remain silent at this time, liberation and rescue will arise for the Jews from another place, and you and your father's house will perish [since you did not help when you had the chance]. And who knows whether you have attained royalty for such a time as this [and for this very purpose]?"

Esther 4:13-14

Esther could have used her position to remain silent or to speak out. She made the hard choice to take a stand for her family and her people by doing the right thing.

Then Esther told them to reply to Mordecai, "Go, gather all the Jews that are present in Susa, and observe a fast for me; do not eat or drink for three days, night or day. I and my maids also will fast in the same way. Then I will go in to [see] the king [without being summoned], which is against the law; and if I perish, I perish."

Esther 4:15-16

On the third day of the fast, Esther put on her royal robes and approached the king and found favor. So much so, that it was to the point of the king being willing to give her up to half of the kingdom.

When the king saw Esther the queen standing in the court, she found favor in his sight; and the king extended to her the golden scepter which was in his hand. So Esther approached and touched the top of the scepter. Then the king said to her, "What is troubling you, Queen Esther? What is your request? It shall be given to you, up to half of the kingdom."

Esther 5:2-3

What I love about Esther is this: although she was afraid, she still managed to step into strength and courage to fulfill her God-ordained destiny. Esther overcame fear, dreading, and self-doubt to step into her role of greatness. She had to get outside of her comfort zone to do so, and the same is true for us.

DO YOU WELL BECAUSE NO ONE ELSE CAN

Work with what He has given you—short, tall, light, dark, curvy, or petite. Just as Queen Esther worked with what she had and found favor in the eyes of her king. Likewise, you will find favor in the eyes of the King of kings when you embrace and work with what He gave you. When God designed you, He did it with a purpose in mind. He gave you gifts, talents, and abilities so you can impact others. Through it all we are blessed, and God gets all the glory. God didn't make a mistake when He designed you. Use what you have to the best of your ability, and allow God to bless your coming in and going out. Allow Him to speak to your heart so you can soar to the heights of your destiny. He will guide you with His wisdom, revelation knowledge, courage, and strength. He will let you know just as he did with Esther whether you need to pray and fast for revelation, deliverance, or to get instruction on your journey. Can you imagine a Jewish orphan girl such as Esther becoming a queen? She wasn't looking for riches or fame. She was living an ordinary life when divinely orchestrated events changed her life. You too are more powerful than you know, and you were designed for greatness.

Prayer of Affirmation

Father, I will give thanks and praise to you, for I am fearfully and wonderfully made; wonderful are Your works, and my soul knows it very well. I am walking out your divine purpose and will for my life in boldness, confidence, and courage in your strength. I need your guidance and ask for the spirit of wisdom and revelation knowledge to be strong upon my life so that I may know you better. I want to be more like Jesus. This is where my true identity rests. I am your workmanship, created in Christ Jesus. Your nature abides in me. As Jesus Christ is, then so am I in this world. Thank you, in Jesus' name. Amen. (Psalm 139:14, Ephesians 1:17, Ephesians 2:10, I John 3:9, I John 4:17)

I EXCEL IN ALL CONTACTS, IN ALL SITUATIONS, AT ALL TIMES IN HIM

And God is able to make all grace abound toward you, that you, always having all sufficiency in all things, may have an abundance for every good work.
2 Corinthians 9:8, NKJV

The devil will try to hinder our walk in the Lord by tripping us up with condemnation and guilt over what we do wrong or over our inabilities and inconsistencies. There are moments when we experience fear and apprehension when dealing with something we think is beyond our reach or capability. For example, too many times I have said no when God was prompting me to take something on, without considering that if God said it, it has to be for my good. When I look back over the times when I've done that it's because I was trying to figure it out on my own. Fear would cause me to ask, "What if I make a mistake? What if I can't figure it out? What will others think?" Asking such questions indicates that I had too much emphasis on self, trying to do things in my own strength.

There were times when I would be guilt-ridden, beating up myself and feeling dejected any time I didn't measure up or I impulsively responded from the flesh. Thoughts like, I thought you were supposed to be a Christian and You said that, invaded my mind. These self-condemning criticisms were rooted in bad teaching. For many years, I thought I had to somehow earn brownie points with God by having good behavior. It was a constant struggle to do right and feel righteous after always making mistakes. Oh my goodness! Can you imagine being on this type of roller coaster? It caused me to be an emotional train wreck. It is important to know the difference between speaking the truth and another thing to do what is right. The former is just words spoken but the latter provides freedom through action.

And you will know the truth [regarding salvation], and the truth will set you free [from the penalty of sin].

John 8:32

THE CAPABILITY TO KNOW TRUTH AND BELIEVE RIGHT

When I began listening to sermons and teachings on God's grace, it was like the light had been turned on in my spirit. It's not about me doing right. It's about believing right.

But to the one who does not work [that is, the one who does not try to earn his salvation by doing good], but believes and completely trusts in Him who justifies the ungodly, his faith is credited to him as righteousness (right standing with God).
Romans 4:5

The Bible clearly states that the moment I believe in Christ, my righteousness is imputed to me by faith, not by works. It takes me from being sin and guilt conscious to Christ-conscious. I am righteous because of the blood of Jesus, because of His finished work on the cross. My faith in what He has already done is counted to me as righteousness. It is a gift from God to me so it's something I must receive by faith!

Through Christ, God sees me as righteous. What a wonderful salvific benefit. As the writer of Hebrews states, "How shall we escape if we neglect so great a salvation?" I'm not confused; I am thankful for my great salvation.

He made Christ who knew no sin to [judicially] be sin on our behalf, so that in Him we would become the righteousness of God [that is, we would be made acceptable to Him and placed in a right relationship with Him by His gracious lovingkindness].
2 Corinthians 5:21

When I think of the goodness of Jesus, it calls to mind the great Christian hymn written by Robert Lowry in 1876, "Nothing but the Blood of Jesus." I remember singing this hymn at my home church so often, and it so ministers to my soul because it conveys the truth about the cleansing power of the blood of Jesus. I want to share the first verse and refrain of this great hymn.

What can wash away my sin
Nothing but the blood of Jesus.
What can make me whole again?
Nothing but the blood of Jesus
(Refrain)

O precious is the flow
That makes me white as snow
No other fount I know
Nothing but the blood of Jesus!

IN NEED OF REGULAR BLOOD BATHS

I thank God for the regular blood bath that keeps on cleansing me from every sin! And because of that, I am always in the light even when I falter. Jesus' blood covers and washes me 24/7 from every sin, so I can keep moving forward strong in the Lord and in the power of His might.

If we [freely] admit that we have sinned and confess our sins, He is faithful and just [true to His own nature and promises], and will forgive our sins and cleanse us continually from all unrighteousness [our wrongdoing, everything not in conformity with His will and purpose].

1 John 1:9

As I shift my focus away from myself, I realize that I can do all things through Christ Jesus who empowers me to do so. The greater one who lives in me guides me with wisdom and revelation knowledge. I excel in all contacts, in all situations, and at all times.

And God is able to make all grace [every favor and earthly blessing] come in abundance to you, so that you may always [under all circumstances, regardless of the need] have complete sufficiency in everything [being completely self-sufficient in Him], and have an abundance for every good work and act of charity.

2 Corinthians 9:8

The pressure is off with me doing anything as I continually believe on Jesus and His saving power, His healing power, and His deliverance power.

Prayer of Affirmation
I am quick to admit when I have sinned and confess my sins, and you are faithful and just, to forgive my sins and cleanse me continually from all unrighteousness. I trust your word that I am forgiven. Now Father, help me to forgive myself. Help me

to keep moving forward strong in you and in the power of Your might. I excel in all contacts, in all situations, and at all times. I'm partnering with the Holy Spirit and where He leads me I will follow with expectation of abounding grace, favor, and blessings in abundance directed toward my life. Your amazing grace causes me to rely on you completely for the good work that I do out of love for You to help advance your kingdom. You will get the absolute glory out of my life. Thank you, in Jesus' name. Amen. (I John 1:9, Ephesians 6:10, 2 Corinthians 9:8)

I AM YIELDED TO GOD AND MY YOUTH IS RENEWED LIKE THE EAGLE'S

Who satisfies your years with good things,
So that your youth is renewed like the [soaring] eagle.
Psalm 103:5

Have you ever been in a situation where your carefully made plans fell through, despite all of your efforts? Have you been qualified for a promotion but you were overlooked only to have it given to someone less qualified? Have you been in a position where you were so close to a breakthrough but something got in the way to block it? This scenario happened to us when we were attempting to purchase a new house. We were so close to moving in that I could taste it. Things seemed to be going as planned when suddenly we were stopped dead in our tracks.

In the fall 2003, Gary and I had been in the process of trying to sell our home as a contingency to purchase a new one. First, we were not getting any offers on our home. That was discouraging by itself. Then after consulting with our mortgage lender we learned that I needed to clear up some credit card debt before moving forward with a home purchase. I was hurt, disappointed, and frustrated. Our credit score was in the 500s. So we devised a plan to get rid of the debt with financial planning and budgeting. I needed to be disciplined in order to get my finances in order.

When I focused in on debt elimination, it took my mind off of purchasing the house so I stopped talking about a house to other people. A lesson learned was that it is not meant for us to expose prematurely our dreams to others. I kept my mouth shut and stopped looking at new homes. This began the process of me enjoying our current home that we were in and being content. Closing the door on past habits that caused incurring credit card debit would be the only way we could move forward. In the mean time, we kept an eye on the interest rates that were steadily dropping to as low as 6.5 percent.

FASTING IS THE WINGS ON PRAYER

On May 23, 2003, I began a 10-day fast asking God for breakthrough with the selling of our home. By this time we had eliminated the credit card debt. However, we still didn't receive any offers to purchase our home until July 7. When Gary came home, he shared what happened with one of our friends. Rose Williams knew that we had our property up for sell, and she had been interceding for us. She also had a property that was up for sell and had recently sold. Therefore, Gary said, "I want to do a 21-day fast and also pray daily for two other couples that have placed their homes on the market to be sold." I told him that I would join him in the fast, because as Scripture says, "One can chase a thousand and two can put ten thousand demons to flight."

That's when a light came on in my mind. I pondered, that in the natural realm when we sow corn, we will reap a harvest of corn. Well, as in the natural, so it is in the spiritual realm. Therefore, I began to utilize the principle of sowing and reaping. For by sowing seeds of prayer for someone's home to sell, we could reap the harvest of our home selling.

For whatever a man sows, that and that only is what he will reap Galatians 6:7.

On July 19, which was the twelfth day of our fast, we finally got a breakthrough with some potential buyers wanting to purchase our home. Yes, Gary and I continued to fast, completing the entire twenty-one days we had committed to. God honored our request by doing exceeding abundantly more than we could ask or think.

Now to Him who is able to [carry out His purpose and] do superabundantly more than all that we dare ask or think [infinitely beyond our greatest prayers, hopes, or dreams], according to His power that is at work within us.
Ephesians 3:20

By yielding to and waiting on God's timing the summer of 2003 was so much better than fall 2002. And the Word of God rang true, "Better is the end of a thing than the beginning of it" (Ecclesiastes 7:8). Here are a few examples of this principle in action:

1. In the fall of 2002 remember I mentioned that I was in debt with credit cards, however in the summer of 2003 we had only use of a debit card.

2. In fall 2002, our credit report rating was in the 500s, however in the summer of 2003 we were in the 600s.
3. The house we were bidding on dropped their initial price, so we got $40,000 in instant equity.
4. Finally, in fall 2002, the interest rate was at 6.5 percent but by the summer of 2003, we locked our interest rate in at 5.75 percent.

On the last day of the 21-day fast, I was thanking and praising God for reaching the conclusion of the fast, when the Lord spoke to my heart, "You were pregnant with a house."

When I looked back in my journal to see the recorded day of our first Open House, it was dated October 12. The bid placed on our house for purchase was July 19, which is exactly nine months. What is also significant is that I was a woman in travail at our intercessory prayer group on July 19 at the same time the potential buyer was looking at our home. Glory to God! God showed up with a miracle in the middle of my mess.

It is indeed as the Word of God says, "But this kind does not go out except by prayer and fasting" (Matthew 17:21). Understand that "this kind" could be anything like disease, unemployment, financial difficulty, marital woes, anger, lying, pending foreclosure, and so on. It is during times like these that we don't magnify the problem, but we magnify the Lord. And if we are under spiritual attack, we must realize that we do not go into the battle alone.

For thou hast girded me with strength unto the battle: thou hast subdued under me those that rose up against me.

Psalm 18:39, KJV

As long as we stand with the Lord during the battle, God will subdue our enemies. We stand protected with the whole armor of God, at times fasting and praying with all prayer and supplication in the spirit. We are to be alert and vigilant, praying at all times.

For the enemy of yours, the devil, roams around like a lion roaring [in fierce hunger], seeking someone to seize upon and devour. Withstand him; be firm in faith [against his onset-rooted, established, strong, immovable, and determined], knowing that the same (identical) sufferings are appointed to your brotherhood (the whole body of Christians) throughout the world.

1 Peter 5:8-9

Even though we all must go through pain and suffering, as Christians we must endure the test of longsuffering. Longsuffering makes us stronger, tougher, and wiser, because we learn to persevere through the trial no matter how long it takes. Though our breakthroughs, visions, and dreams may be delayed, they are not denied. It is of paramount importance that we keep our focus on Jesus, the Author and Finisher of our faith.

For whatever is born of God is victorious over the world; and this is the victory that conquers the world, even our faith. Who is it that is victorious over [that conquers] the world but he who believes that Jesus is the Son of Go [who adheres to, trusts in, and relies on that fact]?

1 John 5: 4-5

We all struggle with our various tests and challenges in life. But remember, we are seated in heavenly places in Christ Jesus. The best place to be is in your seat! Every now and then, we leave our seats. That's to say, we want to take control. Have I gotten out of my seat a time or two (or many) when I yielded to frustration, fear, and worry? Of course! However, whenever I get out of my seat, I come to myself and sit right back down. We are to believe the Word He's given us and praise our way through, pray our way through, and sometimes fast our way through to victory.

Miracles normally manifest with a set of instructions to follow in order to glorify God. What I mean is that sometimes you will have a word from the Lord to follow specifically in order to see your miracle come to pass. We have many examples of this in the Bible. As Moses yielded to God's instruction to "stretch forth his rod," the Red Sea opened up and the Israelites walked through the Red Sea on dry ground!

When Naaman yielded to Elijah's instructions, he received his miracle and was healed of leprosy. "So he went down and plunged himself into the Jordan seven times, just as the man of God had said; and his flesh was restored like that of a little child and he was clean" (2 Kings 5:14). Be encouraged to keep standing on the Word, confessing the Scriptures, and following the instruction given for your miracle breakthrough. You have to believe it and see it happening in the spirit FIRST before you will see manifestation in your life. First Peter 5:10 concludes the matter: After you have suffered for a little while, the God of all grace [who imparts His blessing and favor], who called you to His own eternal glory in Christ, will Himself complete, confirm, strengthen, and establish you [making you what you ought to be].

I want to let you in on a secret. Here's what I have done for a number of years concerning the various testimonies you've have read thus far: I take Scripture and or a prophetic word that someone has given me and stand in my mirror rehearsing what God was doing in my situation, before seeing the manifestation of breakthrough. I envisioned seeing myself standing before people telling them my testimony of healing, deliverance, or a blessing before I got breakthrough. I would rehearse it aloud, from beginning to end like part of a play of how God was going to come through for my situation. Each time I have done it, He has never disappointed me. I give Him all the glory for everything He has done and will do in my life. We are all a continual work in progress. I trust that as we yield ourselves and surrender to His purpose and plan for our lives we will be overtaken with blessings and favor. I am resting on the promise that He satisfies my years with good things, so that my youth is renewed like the eagle.

Who satisfies your years with good things, so that your youth is renewed like the [soaring] eagle.

Psalm 103:5

Prayer of Affirmation

Father, forgive me for the times I have been slow to move on your instructions. I am thankful for you being faithful and the God of another chance that I am able to take heed to your Word. When I am under attack, help me to recognize when I need to fortify my prayer with fasting. Help me to move quickly on your set of instructions with an obedient heart. I bind every hindrance and attack of the enemy coming against my mind, will, finances, body, family, church, ministry, career, business, and relationships, in Jesus name. I need a miracle (in this area—name it). Speak to my heart as I wait on You for wisdom, revelation knowledge, and direction. Speak Lord, I am listening. And I believe You have girded me with strength for the battle. You have subdued under me and caused those who rose up against me to bow down. I stand on your Word in faith, being rooted, established, strong, immovable, and determined. I will endure this test because after I have suffered for a little while, you complete, confirm, strengthen, and establish me. You will make me what I ought to be. I am resting on the promise that He satisfies my years with good things, so that my youth is renewed like the eagle. Thank you, in Jesus' name. Amen. (Matthew 17:21, Psalm 18:39, I Peter 5:8-10, Psalm 103:5)

I AM A PECULIAR PERSON ZEALOUS OF GOOD WORKS AND I HAVE THE ZEAL OF THE LORD IN MY SPIRIT

Who [willingly] gave Himself [to be crucified] on our behalf to redeem us and purchase our freedom from all wickedness, and to purify for Himself a chosen and very special people to be His own possession, who are enthusiastic for doing what is good.
Titus 2:14

Never lagging behind in diligence; aglow in the Spirit, enthusiastically serving the Lord.
Romans 12:11

Have you started out on a journey to fulfill your vision or dream, and then called it quits? Have you been so close to breakthrough then suddenly some sickness, tragedy, or unexpected event brought you to a screeching halt? Did you start a new job, project, or business only to have people ridicule you and tell you that you couldn't do it so you gave up? The passage below reveals how God's people were grappling with being poverty stricken, their homeland becoming rubbish, their self-esteem being shattered, and feelings of utter defeat.

But when Sanballat heard that we were rebuilding the wall, he became furious, completely enraged, and he ridiculed the Jews. He spoke before his brothers and the army of Samaria, "What are these feeble Jews doing? Can they restore it for themselves? Can they offer sacrifices? Can they finish in a day? Can they revive the stones from the heaps of dust and rubbish, even the ones that have been burned?" Now Tobiah the Ammonite was beside him, and he said, "Even what they are building—if a fox should get up on it, he would break down their stone wall." [And Nehemiah prayed] Hear, O our God, how we are despised! Return their taunts on their own heads. Give them up as prey in a land of captivity. Do not forgive their wrongdoing and do not let their sin be wiped out before You, for they have offended the builders [and provoked You]. So we built the wall and the entire wall was joined together to half its height, for the people had a heart to work. But when Sanballat, Tobiah, the Arabs, the Ammonites, and the Ashdodites heard that the repair of the walls of Jerusalem went on, and that the breaches were being closed, they were very angry. They all conspired

together to come and to fight against Jerusalem, and to cause a disturbance in it. But we prayed to our God, and because of them we set up a guard against them day and night. Then [the leaders of] Judah said, "The strength of the burden bearers is failing. And there is much rubble; We ourselves are unable to rebuild the wall."
Nehemiah 4:1-10

However, the passage goes on to say that the people didn't just throw in the towel and settle on wallowing in self-pity. No, they were determined to do something about their situation. They decided to rebuild the wall. Of course, their adversaries heard about it and got very angry with them.

Their situation is indicative of what happens to many of us today. As long as we are going along doing our ordinary work or routine, we are just fine. But the minute we make up our mind to live sold out for God to become the man or woman that God has ordained us to be, then all hell breaks loose to impede our progress. Spiritually, Tobiah, and Sanballat represented the enemy of progress. They attempted to bring ridicule, disappointment, discouragement, and fear, and they threatened force against the efforts of progress.

TALK TO THE HAND

If we're not careful and listen to all the negative talk, we will go from being someone with a winning attitude, convinced of reaching his or her promise land, to being someone who loses momentum to reach our destiny. Due to some adverse circumstances, many people on life's journey have given up on their dreams, visions, ministry, business, relationships, and their God-given purpose along the way. This is why we have to block out criticism and negative talk of haters and not allow that stuff to take root in our hearts. If it does, it will derail you and keep you from fulfilling your assignment. In order to avoid distractions and the pitfalls of haters, you have to distance yourself from anyone that takes you off purpose. Delete these people out of your contact list, and avoid certain places where they hang out. To bring about change for a desired result, we have to do something differently. It is insanity to keep doing the same thing over again but expecting a different result.

In verse 4, we see Nehemiah's immediate course of action was to pray to get instructions from God. We know that the enemy does not fight fair.

Thank God for the spiritual weapons that we have at our disposal. When under attack from Satan, you must fortify yourself with warfare prayer. The enemy will try to disrupt your purpose in life. Satan works through deception and lies to convince believers to give up on their hopes and dreams. Yet the believer's defense and victory against confrontation is to have knowledge of and utilize the Word of God. Therefore, we must be prayerful, maintain a winning attitude, while having confidence and faith in God.

Do not, therefore, fling away your fearless confidence, for it carries a great and glorious compensation of reward.

Hebrews 10:35

Magnify and enlarge God, who holds the solution and minimize the problem. To endure the tests of time and maintain a zeal for the Lord you must have a conqueror's heart and a winning attitude. We must go through tough times and endure battles by staying focused on the fact that God will provide a way of escape. There is no time to get distracted in the heat of the battle. Keep your mind stayed on the Lord.

For you have need of patient endurance [to bear up under difficult circumstances without compromising], so that when you have carried out the will of God, you may receive and enjoy to the full what is promised.

Hebrews 10:36

God is currently building us up and preparing us to possess our promised land and to eventually obtain our destiny. However, we need to do our part by waiting upon the Lord for direction, strength, power, revelation, and divine breakthroughs.

Do not, therefore, fling away your [fearless] confidence, for it has a glorious and great reward.

Hebrews 10:35

All of the troubles and adversities we go through work patience in our life, and abundance and increase in our family relations, marriage, careers, ministry, business, and health. Many people are observing how we respond in tough times. Are we counting it all joy, while going through difficult situations or do we murmur and complain? Paul admonishes us to make this application,

And not only this, but [with joy] let us exult in our sufferings and rejoice in our hardships, knowing that hardship (distress, pressure, trouble) produces patient endurance; and endurance, proven character (spiritual maturity); and proven character, hope and confident assurance [of eternal salvation]. Such hope [in God's promises] never disappoints us, because God's love has been abundantly poured out within our hearts through the Holy Spirit who was given to us (Romans 5: 3-5).

Going back to Nehemiah, verse six goes on to say that after prayer was made, the people remained focused. "But we prayed to our God, and because of them we set up a guard against them day and night" (Nehemiah 4:9). They had a choice to listen to their persecutors or finish the task. Thank God that the people had both a heart and (renewed) mind to work. Noticed my renewed mind emphasis, because the devil's conspiracy and tactics did not cause them to become faint to cease the work.

I looked [them over] and rose up and said to the nobles and officials and the other people. Do not be afraid of the enemy; [earnestly] remember the Lord and imprint Him [on your minds], great and terrible, and [take from Him courage to] fight for your brethren, your sons, your daughters, your wives, and your homes. And when our enemies heard that their plot was known to us and that God had frustrated their purpose, we all returned to the wall, everyone to his work.
Nehemiah 4:14-15

They were all on one accord with intent and focus to complete the work that was before them. The word was given to remember the Lord and imprint Him on your mind and be of good courage. We have to confront and overcome our fears in order to move forward to do the work God has called us to. When we are serious about our calling and begin to take action, God will frustrate the plans of the enemy. So that we are able to complete our assignment to advance the kingdom of God to bring Him glory in the earth realm.

We are already winners, for God causes us to always triumph; therefore, the key is to never let go. Never let go of God's unchanging hand. Never let go in knowing that you come out on the winning side with a victor's attitude being triumphant over your trials and tests. Have an attitude of desperation like Jacob who wrestled with God (the angel of the Lord, or God in angelic form) until daybreak. "But Jacob said, I will not let You go unless You declare a blessing upon me" (Genesis 32:26). Desperation leads people to inconvenience themselves until they get a breakthrough. Jacob's intention was strong in that he refused to let go until he got what he wanted from God.

A breakthrough from heaven at times is born out of a need and desperation to the point where we are willing to sacrifice sleep, food, TV, and so on, until God comes through. Fasting and praying for me has been two of the keys I've utilized over the years to achieve personal victory over strongholds, besetting sins, and other struggles that would attempt to prevent me from springing forward into the promises of God. I repeatedly come to a desperate state where I say, "Enough is enough" and persist until I see breakthrough. I desire to see positive change in my life, family, the household of faith, and many people in the marketplace. It is my constant desire to see people as they really are; not through the lens of my own imperfections, but through the eyes of God. We are an unfinished and imperfect work within ourselves, but well on our way to becoming a masterpiece in Christ Jesus. I rest on the promise that God has never failed me, and I want you to be encouraged that He will never fail you.

I have told you these things, so that in Me you may have [perfect] peace and confidence. In the world you have tribulation and trials and distress and frustration; but be of good cheer [take courage; be confident, certain, undaunted]! For I have overcome the world. [I have deprived it of power to harm you and have conquered it for you].

St. John 16:33

Press on to complete the assignment that has been lying dormant, even if it has been for many years. Press on with courage, confidence, and the strength of Christ empowering you. Rely on the Holy Spirit to give you the first step and then the next step and the following steps. Do not allow the enemy to stop you from pursuing your passion and dreams, because in the end it is not about you.

Position yourself around like-minded people who are in the place where you desire to go. It is all about how you are able to bring glory to His name to help advance His kingdom. Tell the devil these four things:

- I am doing a great work because I am somebody.

- I am not stopping until I complete my assignment because the work is too important.
- I am not quitting because my heart and (renewed) mind are made up. I will allow no one to frustrate my purpose.
- I am a witness that God can resurrect dead dreams and visions and bring them back to life.

Rest on His promises and stay in alignment with the calling He has given you. He's got you covered with the powerful blood of the Lamb. He's got you covered from A-Z. God's got you covered from Genesis to Revelation. Continually abide in Him and rest on His promises. Blessed be the LORD, who has given rest to His people Israel, in accordance with everything that He promised. Not one word has failed of all His good promise, which He spoke through Moses His servant (1 Kings 8:56).

Prayer of Affirmation

I am amazing. I am confident. I am courageous. I am doing a great work because I am somebody. I am not stopping until I complete the assignment you have given me because the work is too important. Lord, I am not quitting because my heart and mind is made up. I can do all things through Christ, who strengthens me. I will not let You go until you declare a blessing upon me. I am a peculiar person zealous of good works, and I have your zeal in my spirit. Abba Daddy, I am resting on your promises, in Jesus' name. Thank you. Amen. (Philippians 4:13, Genesis 32:26, Titus 2:14, Romans 12:11, I Kings 8:56)

Epilogue

And be continually renewed in the spirit of your mind [having a fresh, untarnished mental and spiritual attitude], and put on the new self [the regenerated and renewed nature], created in God's image, [godlike] in the righteousness and holiness of the truth [living in a way that expresses to God your gratitude for your salvation]. Therefore, rejecting all falsehood [whether lying, defrauding, telling half-truths, spreading rumors, any such as these], SPEAK TRUTH EACH ONE WITH HIS NEIGHBOR, for we are all parts of one another [and we are all parts of the body of Christ]. BE ANGRY [at sin—at immorality, at injustice, at ungodly behavior], YET DO NOT SIN; do not let your anger [cause you shame, nor allow it to] last until the sun goes down. And do not give the devil an opportunity [to lead you into sin by holding a grudge, or nurturing anger, or harboring resentment, or cultivating bitterness]. The thief [who has become a believer] must no longer steal, but instead he must work hard [making an honest living], producing that which is good with his own hands, so that he will have something to share with those in need. Do not let unwholesome [foul, profane, worthless, vulgar] words ever come out of your mouth, but only such speech as is good for building up others, according to the need and the occasion, so that it will be a blessing to those who hear [you speak].

Ephesians 4:23-29

This passage of Scripture starts by telling us that due to the constant warring that goes on in the mind, we have to constantly renew our minds to keep a fresh mental and spiritual attitude. Is it easy? No, but it is possible. For some of us it may mean a lifestyle change of being careful what we put before our eye gates and let into our ear gates. "I will set no worthless or wicked thing before my eye" (Psalm101:3). If we permit certain things to penetrate through the gates to our hearts, they will eventually come out of our mouths. Proverbs 4:23 reminds us to "watch over your heart with all diligence, for from it flow the springs of life." Think about all of the life's issues, pain, hurt, and frustration that so many people go through. We should be a spring of water able to provide refreshing to people. Such that when they walk away from a conversation with us they feel refreshed, comforted, and encouraged instead of being more sorrowful.

A renewed mind is sensitive to other peoples feeling and put others before themselves. In honesty, after I began to shift the view off my self-interest, selfishness, and self-pity my heart became undone for others. I've found that being determined to think on ways to help, encourage, pray, and bless others that God helps me concerning my personal issues. We can never go wrong as we become doers of God's Word.

Make my joy complete by being of the same mind, having the same love [toward one another], knit together in spirit, intent on one purpose [and living a life that reflects your faith and spreads the gospel—the good news regarding salvation through faith in Christ]. Do nothing from selfishness or empty conceit [through factional motives, or strife], but with [an attitude of] humility [being neither arrogant nor self-righteous], regard others as more important than yourselves. Do not merely look out for your own personal interests, but also for the interests of others. Have this same attitude in yourselves which was in Christ Jesus [look to Him as your example in selfless humility].

Philippians 2:2-5

I must admit that I've spent many months and years in certain areas of my life in the wilderness struggling. Why? Because when under attack I let my little member get me in trouble, I would second guess myself, or I would be stubborn and rebellious. I then had to make the choice to repent, ask God for forgiveness, forgive myself, and if needed go to others and ask for their forgiveness. One thing I've settled on is to never give up or give in to the devil concerning myself, family, and those I intercede for on a daily basis.

I've learned that this is a spiritual fight, and I've gone through a lot of tests in this area. I've been able to write and share from personal testimony some of the breakthroughs and deliverance that were needed in my life. When I got fed up with my condition, out of desperation I turned to God. A vital key is surrendering to the Lord with prayer and fasting.

Then you will call on Me and you will come and pray to Me, and I will hear [your voice] and I will listen to you. Then [with a deep longing] you will seek Me and require Me [as a vital necessity] and [you will] find Me when you search for Me with all your heart.

Jeremiah 29:12-13

Seeking God and drawing closer to Him in relationship, renewing your mind, daily meditation on the Word, praising your way through, and speaking the Word aloud in faith will lead you to victory.

Be encouraged to stay connected to the truth of God's Word and abide in His presence. The Word of God will give you a better outlook of your future, dreams, vision, and destiny. He came as a giver of abundant life and that you would prosper holistically. "Beloved, I pray that you may prosper in every way and [that your body] may keep well, even as [I know] your soul keeps well and prospers" (3 John 2). God desires to fulfill His purpose in you. You'll experience peace, healing, joy, goodness, and many benefits keeping your eyes focused on the author and finisher of your faith. Refuse to waddle in the ashes and rubbish of past failures and mistakes. Have a made-up mind that is renewed and stayed on Christ Jesus. Be determined to seek God's purpose for your life and continue to go forward in Him. God has destined a life for you full of blessings and fruitfulness.

"For I know the plans and thoughts that I have for you," says the LORD, "plans for peace and well-being and not for disaster to give you a future and a hope."
Jeremiah 29:11

And the blessing doesn't stop with you, but it should continue to reach out to impact the lives of many others connected to you by assignment or gifted to you by birth. You should also leave a legacy for your children and grandchildren to be carried on and maintained from generation to generation. "A good man leaves an inheritance to his children's children, and the wealth of the sinner is stored up for [the hands of] the righteous" (Proverbs 13:22). Rest on His promises. God has got you covered…from A-Z…from Genesis to Revelation.

About the Author

Lauretha Ward attends Burning Bush International Ministries in Ypsilanti, where Bishop Don W. Shelby Jr, is Founder & Pastor. She is a gifted and anointed author, intercessor, and teacher. Lauretha says, "Prayer and Fasting is a vital part of my life and has wrought personal breakthrough, healing, deliverance, miracles, and increase. More importantly as an intercessor I have witnessed the power of answered prayer for the churched and un-churched. My desire and ambition is to encourage and demonstrate God's love to others."

Professionally, Mrs. Ward is a Speech-Language Pathologist and has a heart for seeing restoration, salvation, and healing take place in the lives of her clients. She has been the wife of Dr. Gary Ward since 1992, and they are the parents of two sons, Aaron and Laurence. Lauretha counts it a blessing to live a purpose driven life. The purpose of this ministry is to equip and empower individuals with how to have breakthrough during tough times through the Word of God. Lauretha says, "my aim is to share the message that God has given me for His people on how to be changed inside-out while learning to find comfort, encouragement, and hope during life's challenges; stimulate and promote faith in the hearts of the believers; and inspire a deeper devotion to Christ." But grow in grace (undeserved favor, spiritual strength) and recognition and knowledge and understanding of our Lord and Savior Jesus Christ (the Messiah)…" 2 Peter 3:18.

About the Publisher

Let *Life to Legacy* bring your story to literary life! We offer the following publishing services: manuscript development, editing, transcription services, ghostwriting, cover design, copyright services, ISBN assignment, worldwide distribution, and eBook conversion.

We make the publishing process easy. Throughout production, we keep the author informed every step of the way. Even if you do not have a manuscript, that's not a problem for us. We can ghostwrite your book from audio recordings or legible handwritten documents. Whether print-on-demand or trade publishing, we have packages to meet your publishing needs. At *Life to Legacy*, we take the stress out of becoming a published author.

Unlike other *so-called* publishers, we do more than just print books. Our books and eBooks are distributed to book buyers, distributors, and online retailers throughout the world—this is real publishing! Call us today for a free quote.

Please visit our website
www.Life2Legacy.com

or call us
877-267-7477

Send e-mail inquiries
Life2Legacybooks@att.net

www.ingramcontent.com/pod-product-compliance
Lightning Source LLC
Chambersburg PA
CBHW032127090426
42743CB00007B/496